# CRITICAL ACCL<

# THE WORKS OF JAM]

MW01133834

### Saving Shallmar

"But Saving Shallmar's Christmas story is a tale of compassion and charity, and the will to help fellow human beings not only survive, but also be ready to spring into action when a new opportunity presents itself. Bittersweet yet heartwarming, Saving Shallmar is a wonderful Christmas season story for readers of all ages and backgrounds, highly recommended."

*Small Press Bookwatch*

### Battlefield Angels

"Rada describes women religious who selflessly performed life-saving work in often miserable conditions and thereby gained the admiration and respect of countless contemporaries. In so doing, Rada offers an appealing narrative and an entry point into the wealth of sources kept by the sisters."

*Catholic News Service*

### Between Rail and River

"The book is an enjoyable, clean family read, with characters young and old for a broad-based appeal to both teens and adults. Between Rail and River also provides a unique, regional appeal, as it teaches about a particular group of people, ordinary working 'canawlers' in a story that goes beyond the usual coverage of life during the Civil War."

*Historical Fiction Review*

### Canawlers

"A powerful, thoughtful and fascinating historical novel, Canawlers documents author James Rada, Jr. as a writer of considerable and deftly expressed storytelling talent."

*Midwest Book Review*

"James Rada, of Cumberland, has written a historical novel for high-schoolers and adults, which relates the adventures, hardships and ultimate tragedy of a family of boaters on the C&O Canal. … The tale moves quickly and should hold the attention of readers looking for an imaginative adventure set on the canal at a critical time in history."

*Along the Towpath*

## OTHER BOOKS BY JAMES RADA, JR.

*Fiction*

Beast

Between Rail and River (Canawlers #2)

Canawlers (Canawlers #1)

Kachina*

Kuskurza*

Lock Ready (Canawlers #3)

Logan's Fire

My Little Angel

The Race (a Canawlers story)

The Rain Man

October Mourning


*Non-Fiction*

Battlefield Angels: The Daughters of Charity Work as Civil War Nurses

Beyond the Battlefield: Stories from Gettysburg's Rich History

Echoes of War Drums: The Civil War in Mountain Maryland

Kidnapping the General: The South's Most-Daring Raid Against the Union Army*

Looking Back: True Stories of Mountain Maryland

Looking Back II: More True Stories of Mountain Maryland

Saving Shallmar: Christmas Spirit in a Coal Town

When the Babe Came to Town: Stories of George Herman Ruth's Small-Town Baseball Games*

* e-book only

# THE LAST TO FALL

## The 1922 March, Battles, & Deaths
## of U.S. Marines at Gettysburg

by

Richard D. L. Fulton & James Rada, Jr.

### LEGACY

PUBLISHING

## Dedicated in memory of

**Capt. George W. Hamilton and GySgt. George R. Martin**
Who perished in the line of duty at Gettysburg, June 26, 1922, and who were *The Last to Fall*.

*And to...*

Cathe Adelsberger-Fulton, wife of co-author Richard D. L. Fulton,
who served as the research assistant and editor for *The Last to Fall*

Marine Pfc. Ben C. Rada, son of co-author James Rada, Jr.,
who graduated from Parris Island, 2015.

THE LAST TO FALL:
THE 1922 MARCH, BATTLES, & DEATHS OF U.S. MARINES AT GETTYSBURG

Published by Legacy Publishing, a division of AIM Publishing Group.
Gettysburg, Pennsylvania.
Copyright © 2015 by Richard D. L. Fulton & James Rada, Jr.
All rights reserved.
Printed in the United States of America.
First printing: April 2015.

ISBN 978-0692413425

LEGACY
PUBLISHING

315 Oak Lane • Gettysburg, Pennsylvania 17325

# CONTENTS

The strangest thing about them was they moved without seeming to move. No motion of their legs or bodies could be detected from the old Union lines. They seemed to be rolling across like figures on an escalator, as though the ground itself was bearing them forward while they stood still. And there was so many of them... like parading battalions of ghosts.

*– The (Baltimore) Sun,*
July 2, 1922[1]

# PREFACE

# WHAT IF?

Confederate M1917 tanks lumber across the fields, moving on the Union position behind a stone wall on Cemetery Ridge in Gettysburg, Pa. The Union soldiers fire machine guns not so much at the massive metal vehicles approaching them, but at the Confederate soldiers using the tanks as cover in order to make their way across the open ground. In the face of an unstoppable weapon, the Union soldiers begin falling back.

Hearing loud buzzing sounds from above, the Confederates stare upward as Union de Havilland DH-4B biplanes fly out of the clouds. The airplanes level off safely out of range of the Confederate rifle fire. Then the explosions commence as the bombs rain down around the tanks and troops turning General Pickett's Charge into a bloodbath.

**Pages 8-9:** Marines charge the High Water Mark, Gettysburg battlefield, 1922. **Page 10 Top: A** *de* Havilland DH4 dive bomber flying over France in 1918. The DH4 was the precursor of the DH-4B dive bombers used by the Marines during the Gettysburg battlefield exercises in 1922. **Page 10 Bottom:** M1917 tanks attack alongside of Marine infantry during maneuvers at Quantico in 1924. The same type of tanks had been deployed on the Gettysburg battlefield two years earlier. **Above:** A veteran of the American Civil War shares his experiences with a Marine at the High Water Mark in the Gettysburg National Military Park during the 1922 maneuvers.

It's not science fiction. Something very similar actually happened in 1922.

The slaughter of the 1863 Battle of Gettysburg ended the Confederate invasion of Pennsylvania, but after the Allied victory of World War I, people began to wonder what if some of the post-world war military technology had been available during the American Civil War?

Marine officers debating these questions after the end of WWI had the capability to test their theories. The maneuvers were meant to train in a realistic battle substituting "modern-day" military equipment for that which had been used during the Civil War.

On June 19, 1922, more than 5,000 Marines left Quantico, heading north to the battlefield of Gettysburg. While some injuries had been expected as was the case with any large battle simulation, men died during these maneuvers becoming the last U.S. Marines killed in the line of duty on the Gettysburg battlefield.

Despite the pall cast over the maneuvers following the deaths, the Marine mission proceeded. For 10 days, battle raged once again on the fields and ridges where thousands had perished 59 years prior... climaxing on July 4 when the Marines fought the Battle of Gettysburg... with "modern" weapons and tactics.

"They are so busy keeping in trim: they are learning new things themselves and making real marines out of the 'boots' and the 'baby officers.' They have weighty problems on their chests. When the time comes to make more history, the marines want to be the first to start."

– *The (Baltimore) Sun*
June 25, 1922[1]

# FIRST TO FIGHT

"DEMOCRACY'S VANGUARD"

# U·S·MARINE CORPS

## JOIN NOW AND TEST YOUR COURAGE
## REAL FIGHTING WITH REAL FIGHTERS

APPLY AT

24 EAST 23rd STREET, NEW YORK

# CHAPTER 1

# AT QUANTICO

Unlike the gallant image held by our present-day United States Marines, the Marines of the 1860's were a small group of fighting men. With fewer than 3,000 men and lacking strong leadership, Marines served in a sideline role during the Civil War. Their primary duties were guarding ships and forts, although some Marines did participate in the First Battle of Bull Run and the attacks on New Orleans, Charleston, and Fort Fisher.[2]

Sometimes it appeared that military officers and political figures seemed to be at a loss regarding the most-beneficial strategy and placement of the Marines. The Marines had fought valiantly in World War I like in the Battle of Belleau Wood in France. After the deadly fighting there to drive the entrenched German troops from the Wood, Army General John J. Pershing, commander of the American Expeditionary Force, said, "The deadliest weapon in the world is a Marine and his rifle."[3]

However, that didn't stop Pershing and others from wanting to disband the Marine Corps after the war had been won.

"Right after World War I, when John A. Lejeune was appointed commandant of the Marine Corps, there was a push by General Pershing and President Wilson to have the Marine Corps abolished," said Gunnery Sergeant Thomas Williams, executive director of the United States Marine Corps Historical Company.[4]

It wasn't the first time such an action had been considered, nor would it be the last. However, Major General Lejeune, commandant of the Marine Corps, was a Marine through and through, and he wasn't going to go down without a fight.

Lejeune understood that this was a political battle that would be fought on the battlefield of public opinion. He devised a campaign to raise public awareness about the Marine Corps just as the government had rallied public opinion behind the troops during the war.

A number of things evolved from this effort. Celebrating the birthday of the Marine Corps as November 10, 1775 was part of the public relations push by the Marine Corps. Also, elements of the Marine uniform were tied to iconic battles or moments of Marine Corps history.[5]

Gen. Lejeune also wanted to improve the skills

**Pages 12-13:** Marine recruits arrive at Quantico, circa 1918. **Page 14 Top:** Quantico, 1920. *Page 14 Poster:* "First to Fight." **Above:** Union Marines at Washington, D.C. Navy Yard, 1864.

and abilities of the Corps by applying lessons learned from WWI to introduce new tactical doctrines. He realized that he could do this and use it as a means of increasing public awareness about the Marine Corps.

"Instead of going to obscure places to conduct war games and learning lessons learned and learning how to integrate armor, artillery, and aviation into war fighting, he would do it at iconic places and put the Marines out in front of the public," Williams said.

At the time, the national military parks, such as Gettysburg, were still under control of the U.S. War Department, which meant the Marines could use the parks as a training ground. Lejeune chose to do just that with a series of annual training exercises, which commenced in 1921.

## Quantico

Forty miles south of Washington, D.C., Quantico sits along the Quantico Creek, a tributary of the Potomac River. The creek gives the "Sea Soldiers" both easy access to the waterways and the name of the headquarters.

Quantico Creek had been used as a trading center for centuries, but it wasn't until the early twentieth century that it was looked at as a location for a Marine base. A group of officers and officials toured the site on April 18, 1917, and on April 23 reported that "it is believed that the site at Quantico fulfills all requirements of a concentration and training camp for the Marine Corps, and all the requirements for a permanent post, except that it is not on deep water."[6]

Once the decision was made to use the site, tent buildings were quickly erected and by August, the tents had been replaced with wooden buildings and barracks set along squared-off streets.

In June 1917, the first aviation unit, Squadron C Marine Aviation Force, arrived and set up an airfield on what would become Brown Field four years later.

Quantico experienced a number of different commanders in its early years as officers were moved in and out of the camp to service in WWI. General Smedley Butler assumed command of the Marine Barracks Quantico at the end of June 1920 and it was his idea to stage the Civil War exercises. He "envisioned Civil War reenactments as a means not only to provide a proving ground for innovations in the Corps, but as a way to increase publicity for a Marine Corps which was suffering from the effects of the drawdown that followed World War I."[7]

In fact, it was expected that the U.S. Congress would decide on how large the Corps should be and appropriate the necessary funds during July 1922. The Corps had seen its numbers drop drastically in recent years from its 1918 high of 75,101 enlisted men and 2,882 officers. The maximum strength that it had been authorized that year was 75,500 enlisted men and 3,200 officers. The 1921 appropriation allowed for a maximum corps of 21,000 enlisted men, less than a third of what it had been during the war.[8]

## Replaying the Civil War

In late September 1921, nearly 5,000 Marines, including the Fifth and Sixth Marine Regiments (infantry); Tenth Marine Regiment (artillery); battalions of attached engineers, signalers, and medical corps; and detachments of aviation and chemical units marched from Quantico to Fredericksburg to conduct training exercises.

It was an event that the Marines played up in the press, trying to attract as much attention to it as they could. It attracted attention across the nation, in part because of the size of the group marching through Virginia. *The (Gettysburg) Star and Sentinel* called it the greatest military maneuvers under the flag in a time of peace.[9]

The march from Quantico began on Monday, September 26, 1921. Each Marine carried a pack weighing 87 pounds, not including his rifle and oth-

"Bird's Eye" view of Marine Corps Base Quantico, 1918.

# MAJOR GENERAL JOHN A. LEJEUNE

Maj. Gen. John A. Lejeune, holding medals.

Maj. Gen. John A. Lejeune has been called "the greatest of all Leathernecks" and a "Marine's Marine." Born in Louisiana in 1867, he was the son of a Confederate Army captain. He graduated from the U.S. Naval Academy in 1888, second in his class of 32. However, after serving two years as a Navy midshipman, he decided that he would rather be a Marine. He joined the Corps as a second lieutenant in 1890.

He commanded the Marine Guard on the U.S.S. Cincinnati during the Spanish-American War. He then continued on to command Marines attached to a number of different ships in places like the Philippines, Mexico, Cuba, and Panama. All the while, he continued earning promotions for his service and leadership.

During World War I, he served with distinction in France, earning the Legion of Honor and the Croix de guerre from France, the U.S. Army Distinguished Service Medal, and the U.S. Navy Distinguished Service Medal.

In October 1919, he was appointed as the commanding general of the Quantico Marine Barracks for a second time. (He had also held that position for a short time at the beginning of WWI.)

He became the Major General Commandant of the Marine Corps on July 1, 1920. He served in that post until 1929.

Upon his retirement from the Marine Corps, he became the superintendent of the Virginia Military Institute and served until 1937.

He died on November 20, 1942, at the Union Memorial Hospital in Baltimore, Maryland. He was interred at Arlington National Cemetery.

er equipment. They hiked 10 miles that first day and soaked their aching feet and enjoyed movies in the evening.[10] Though 10 miles wasn't a particularly long march, doing so while essentially carrying half of their bodyweight on their backs wore them out quickly.

They slept in small two-man tents. "Our beds were a little different from what we had been accustomed to, being of 'Mother Earth and rocks.' I thought my hip bones were going to come thru several times before morning," wrote Leo S. Phillips, a Marine on the march.[11]

The following day's hike was another 14 miles with about half of it marched in the rain. The Marines arrived at the Fredericksburg fair grounds exhausted, but their spirits brightened as the town band greeted them. Their camp had been set up next to an on-going fair and many of the Marines spent the evening playing games on the midway or enjoying the rides.[12]

The next day was a short hike to the Wilderness battlefield. It should have been easy, but the day was unseasonably hot and the men were tired. Marines started falling behind. Ambulances picked up those Marines who were the most-affected by the heat and other ailments and treated them. Sadly, three Marines died on the last leg of the march.[13]

When the Marines arrived in Camp Harding, named for the president who would be coming to watch their war games, they were tired and thirsty. They were told that they couldn't have water until their tents were up.

"Well, you should have seen the tent poles and pins flying," Phillips said.[14]

The next four days were spent practicing tactics on the battlefield and participating in war games. Their goal wasn't to reenact the Battle of the Wilderness so much as give the training exercises an older feel to them. However, when the modern

**Above:** Marine 75mm gun and caisson being hauled by military tractor at the 1921 Wilderness, Virginia, maneuvers. **Below:** Marines en route to the 1921 Wilderness, Virginia, maneuvers.

equipment took to the field, there was no mistaking that it was a demonstration of America's military might, which had recently helped win The War to End All Wars.

Since another goal of the maneuvers was to gain positive publicity for the Marine Corps, Gen. Butler had invited President Warren G. Harding to review the troops. The president and first lady drove down from Washington, D.C. to Camp Harding on Saturday, October 1, 1921. He was joined by a number of other dignitaries who drove from Washington, D.C. to observe the exercises.

"Before the President's interested eyes swung an observation navy blimp. Airplanes with bombers and observers hummed above them. The steady drum of machine guns rolled from slope to slope. One-fifty-fives and 75's threw out an incessant cannonade. Tanks tore their way through the undergrowth. The First, Fifth, Sixth, and Tenth Regi-

ments of marines were the mimic contenders," *The Washington Post* reported.[15]

Apparently Harding got caught up in the excitement of the mock battle and left his safe vantage point to go down on the field and walk among the Marines. Generals Lejeune and Butler accompanied him, providing a running commentary on what was happening as they walked along behind the Marines.

"For nearly a mile across the theoretically bullet-swept expanse the president kept pace with the onrushing Marines.

"He was glad when the 'enemy' was reached and vanquished and the order to 'cease firing' was passed down the line. His neat brown suit was dusty, he was ruddy-faced and down his cheeks trickled small streams of perspiration," *The Ogden (Utah)Standard Examiner* reported.[16]

While in camp, Harding met with a handful of Civil War veterans; six former Confederate soldiers and four former Union soldiers. They shook hands with the president and posed for pictures with him.[17]

The president and Florence Harding spent the night in a large canvas "White House" that had been constructed especially for the Hardings so that it had all of the modern conveniences. It was the first time Florence Harding had ever spent the night in a tent and the first time a president had spent the night in a camp with troops since the Civil War.[18]

The next morning the Hardings ate breakfast with the Marines and then attended a religious service with them.

Afterwards, Harding told the group, "It was suggested that I stand here before you mainly that we might be better acquainted. After all it is ours to serve together. I cannot tell you how inspiring it had been to sit in worship with you and how greatly I have enjoyed being in camp with you. I shall not exaggerate a single word when I tell you that from my boyhood to the present hour I have always had a very profound regard for the United States Marines, and I am leaving camp today with that regard strengthened and genuine affection added."[19]

The president and his guests headed back to Washington later in the day and the Marines started on their march back to Quantico the following day. By the time they arrived back in Quantico, seven Marines had died during the exercises and one had been wounded by a hand grenade.[20]

The main purpose of the maneuvers had been achieved and the Marines had additionally gained some influential friends and a great deal of positive publicity.

General Smedley Darlington Butler at the Wilderness maneuvers, 1921.

# MAJOR GENERAL SMEDLEY D. BUTLER

General Smedley Butler in camp en route to Gettysburg, 1922.

Born in West Chester, Pa., in 1881, Smedley Butler was commissioned as a probationary second lieutenant at the age of 17 in 1898. He trained at the Old Marine Barracks in Washington, D.C. before being sent to fight in the Spanish-American War in Cuba.

During the following years, he moved from one action to another. He fought in the Philippine insurrection in Orani in 1899, and then the Boxer Rebellion in China. He was wounded in the latter action and brevetted to the rank of captain for his gallantry. He served in Culebra in 1902, and Panama 1903-1904.

Things settled down for a few years after this, but from 1910 to 1914 he returned to Panama to command Camp Elliott and lead an expedition to Nicaragua. In April 1914, he was involved in the occupation of Vera Cruz and was awarded his first Medal of Honor.

The following year, he received his second Medal of Honor during an expedition to Haiti. He organized and commanded the native Haitien Gendarmerie from 1916 to 1918.

At the end of WWI, he took the 13th Regiment of Marines to France where he commanded Camp Pontanezen Barracks at Brest.

He assumed command of Marine Barracks Quantico in 1920. He was promoted to major general in 1929.

By the time Butler retired from active duty in 1931, he had received 16 medals, including five for heroism. He is the only Marine to ever be awarded the Marine Corps Brevet Medal and two Medals of Honor.

# USMC Civil War Training Exercises

| Battle | Location | Battle Date | USMC Exercises |
|---|---|---|---|
| The Wilderness | Spotsylvania Co., VA | May 5-7, 1864 | 1921 |
| Battle of Gettysburg | Gettysburg, PA | July 1-3, 1863 | 1922 |
| New Market | New Market, VA | May 15, 1864 | 1923 |
| Antietam | Sharpsburg, MD | September 17, 1862 | 1924 |
| Chancellorsville | Chancellorsville, VA | April 30-May 6, 1863 | 1935 |
| Manassas | Manassas, VA | July 21, 1861 | 1936 |
| Petersburg | Petersburg, VA | June 9, 1864-March 25, 1865 | 1937 |

Capture of Fort Riviere, Haiti, November 17, 1915, featuring Major Smedley Butler at center (flanked by Sergeant Ross Iams at left and Private Samuel Gross at right), as depicted by artist Donna J. Neary.

"There would be something pathetic in the thought that the Fifth and Sixth regiments of Marines, that did so much to turn the tide in 1918, when it most needed turning, should be out on the highways pleading silently with the people who used to worship them not to let the politicians throw them on the scrap heap. It would be pathetic if it weren't for the fact that when you see them trekking along the highroad, pathos is the last thing that enters your soul, because it seems to be so far away from their own souls."

— *The (Baltimore) Sun,*
*June 25, 1922*[1]

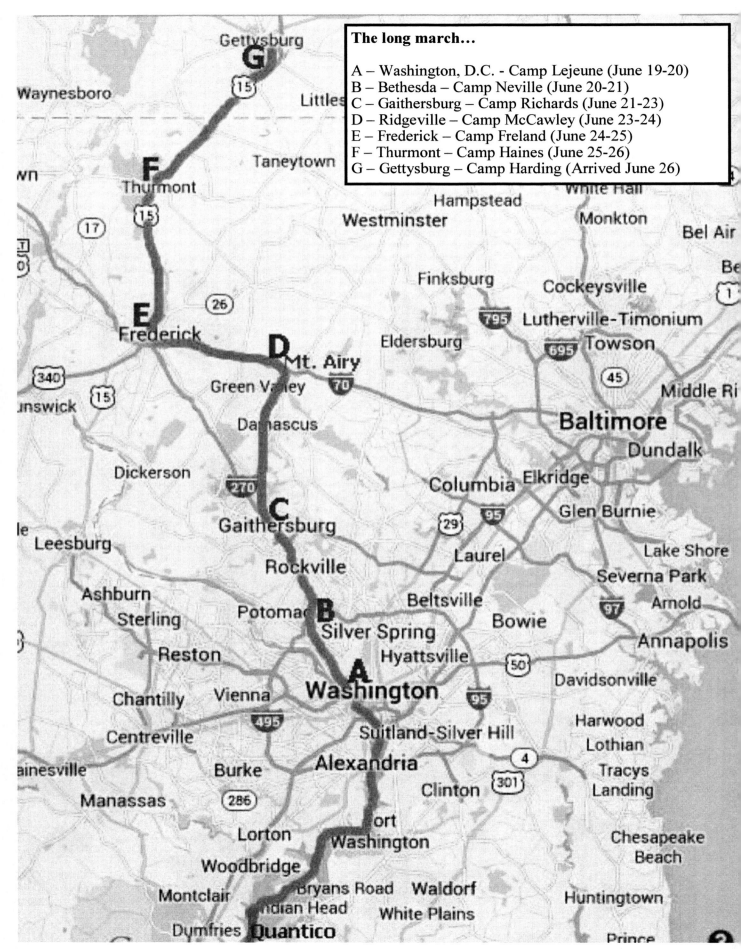

The long march...

A – Washington, D.C. - Camp Lejeune (June 19-20)
B – Bethesda – Camp Neville (June 20-21)
C – Gaithersburg – Camp Richards (June 21-23)
D – Ridgeville – Camp McCawley (June 23-24)
E – Frederick – Camp Freland (June 24-25)
F – Thurmont – Camp Haines (June 25-26)
G – Gettysburg – Camp Harding (Arrived June 26)

# CHAPTER 2

# THE LONG MARCH

Early in the morning of Monday, June 19, 1922, thousands of Marines at the Marine Camp Quantico – roughly a quarter of the Corps – marched from their barracks down to the dock along Quantico Creek, a tidal tributary of the Potomac River. There, the East Coast Expeditonary Force filed onto waiting barges supplied by the U.S. Navy as "one of the greatest and most comprehensive of troop maneuvers in the history of the United States in time of peace began."[2]

The scope of the 1922 maneuvers dwarfed the previous year's march to Fredericksburg. General Smedley Butler had traveled the route of the 1922 march to ensure that it would suit the needs of the Marines. He had even made his very first flight in an airplane to visit Gettysburg and plan out the Marines' time there.[3]

At 4 a.m., four Navy tug boats towed eight large barges up the Potomac River toward Washington,

D.C.[4] They passed Mount Vernon, home of the first president, and Alexandria, Va., the port town. It was a path that the Union Army had always feared the Confederate Navy would take to invade Washington, D.C. during the Civil War. Only now, it was being undertaken by an invading Union Army.

Meanwhile, tanks and artillery pieces towed by trucks rolled out along the Richmond Road headed for the same destination. Unlike a typical invasion, the Marines gave consideration to any possible damage they might cause to the roads. They removed the steel cleats and spikes from the tractor and tank treads. Only the smooth steel under-surface of the belts would be in contact with the road.[5]

The march involved the entire Fifth and Sixth Regiments, a squadron of the First Marine Air Wing, and elements of the Tenth Marine Artillery.[6] *The (Baltimore) Sun* noted that these Marines were ready for anything and had pretty much cleaned out Quantico of anything that could be moved.[7] "The 5,000 men are carrying the equipment of a complete division of nearly 20,000. In the machine-gun outfits especially the personnel is skeletonized, while the material is complete. Companies of 88 men are carrying ammunition, range finders and other technical gear for companies of about 140."[8]

**Pages 22-23:** Marines march down North Market Street, Frederick, Md., June 24, on their march to Gettysburg. They are passing the same place as General Smedley Butler on pge 40. **Page 24:** Map of Marine march to Gettysburg, 1922. **Above:** East Potomac Park, Washington, D.C., aerial view from above Hains Point, looking north toward the National Mall. The Marine barracks are located at the upper right portion of the island, just before the bridge.

**Above:** Docks on Potomac River, Marine Corps Base, Quantico, Virginia, circa 1920s. **Page 27 Top:** Marines setting up camp at East Potomac Park (dubbed Camp Lejeune) June 19 before leaving the island to be reviewed by the president at the White House. **Page 27 Bottom:** Marine Camp Lejeune encampment at East Potomac Park (Marine Barracks Washington).

### East Potomac Park

The barges arrived at the sea wall at East Potomac Park, south of the Washington Monument at noon and the Marines began setting up their camp, which took about two hours. "When the head of the column of guns, lorries and wagons reached the edges of the Capital the tail of it was still at Quantico," *The Sun* reported.[9] This meant that on this first day of travel, the line of equipment vehicles stretched out for 35 miles, indicating that some of the equipment was slow in getting started on the journey.

Gen. Butler's headquarters was set up on the north side of the park facing the wharves.

The trucks and tanks began arriving at the park at 12:30, but were left parked along the road on the southern end of the long bridge crossing the Potomac River from Virginia to Washington.

East Potomac Park is home to many of the cherry trees that Tokyo Mayor Yukio Ozaki donated to Washington in 1912. Kwanzan cherry blossom

trees that produced clusters of clear pink double blossoms, Fugenzo trees that produced rosy pink double blossoms, and Shirofugen trees that produced white double blossoms that age to pink could all be seen within the park. Though the first Cherry Blossom Festival was still more than a decade away, the beautiful trees nonetheless attracted countless tourists in the spring.

The Marines were more interested in the open park land on the peninsula of land than the view. More than 5,000 Marines and more than 1,000 pieces of motorized equipment were at the camp, which was named Camp Lejeune, following Gen. Butler's practice of naming camps after Marine Corps generals.

Although the park had been used to house soldiers during World War I, it had once been swamp land that apparently was not all that solid in areas. "They are camping on reclaimed land, and they found out when they landed here from Quantico, Va., this morning, that some of it hadn't been fully reclaimed. Some spots that looked like fine tenting grounds on the map turned out to be swamp. But

# East Potomac Park

Since much of the area of Washington, D.C. is a drained swamp, it is not surprising that flooding had caused on-going problems whenever the Potomac River overflowed its banks. As the city's population grew and buildings and monuments were built on any available land, it became particularly troublesome. In a 20-year span from 1870 to 1890, the city experienced four major floods. These floods were deep enough that rowboats were necessary for traveling up and down Pennsylvania Avenue.[11]

After a flood in 1881, the U.S. Army Corps of Engineers dredged a deeper channel in the Potomac River, allowing it to handle a greater water flow. The engineers used the dredged-up material to raise the land along Pennsylvania Avenue and around the White House.[12]

Although the work to create the park was done out of necessity for sanitation and harbor improvements, it was also known that a new park would be one of the positive benefits of all of this work.[13]

Potomac Park was completed on March 3, 1897. It would eventually become West Potomac Park as a new land reclamation project that would become East Potomac Park was undertaken.

The U.S. Senate formed the Senate Park Commission in 1901 to reconcile competing visions for future development of the city.[14] The commission became known as the McMillan Commission, named after Republican Senator James McMillan of Michigan, who was the commission chairman.

The commission's plan, released in 1902, called for East Potomac Park to be turned into a formal park that included recreation facilities. As the dredging of the Potomac River continued, the material was built up to form a new section of land. In 1911, a road was constructed around the perimeter of the park and cherry trees, a gift from Japan in 1912, were planted along the roadway by the inspiration and direction of First Lady Helen Taft, wife of President William Howard Taft.

Temporary soldiers' barracks were constructed on the land during WWI as were victory gardens. Both of these had disappeared by the arrival of the Marines in 1922.

East Potomac Park now remains as it was then, a scenic park on the edge of the National Mall, especially popular in the spring when the world-renowned cherry blossoms are in bloom.

Photographers and painters along the Tidal Basin under blossoming cherry trees, 1920 .

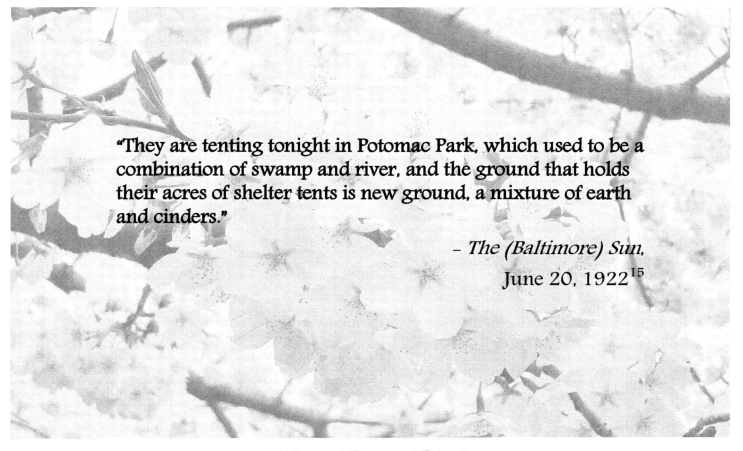

"They are tenting tonight in Potomac Park, which used to be a combination of swamp and river, and the ground that holds their acres of shelter tents is new ground, a mixture of earth and cinders."

*– The (Baltimore) Sun,*
*June 20, 1922*[15]

# What They Took

Here is a partial list of the equipment taken on the 1922 march to Gettysburg as reported in *The (Baltimore) Sun.*[16] As extensive as this list is, it is incomplete with two obvious gaps being the thirty airplanes and four tanks that were also part of the maneuvers:

- 279 machine gun carts
- 31 trailer kitchens
- 26 tank trailers
- 24 artillery trains
- 71 motorcycles
- 13 touring cars
- 40 bicycles
- 70 horses
- 12 mules
- 3 large ambulances
- 11 small ambulances
- 4 radio trucks

- 7 staff reconnaissance cars
- 49 trailers
- 100 heavy trucks
- 6 light trucks
- 3 small trucks
- 4 gas trucks
- 3 combat trucks
- 2 derrick trucks
- 4 repair trucks
- 4 listening trucks
- 4 ten-ton trucks
- 38 five-ton trucks

# A PRESIDENTIAL REVIEW

"They captured the White House, which was easy, the gates being thrown open and the President of the United States, his Cabinet and a battalion of Senators and Representatives who were massed upon the south portico, putting up little in the way of a struggle.

"For the first time since the Civil War, armed forces in Uniform and fighting equipment marched across the White House Lawns."

*– The (Baltimore) Sun*, June 20, 1922[17]

**Below:** The Marine Band, a combining of the Fifth, Sixth, and Tenth Regimental Bands, performing for President and First Lady Harding on June 19 at the White House. **Page 31 Top:** Marines passing in review at the White House on June 19 before their march to Gettysburg. **Page 31 Bottom:** Marine color guard leaving the White House grounds on June 19 after being reviewed by President and First Lady Harding.

# Charles I. Corby

Born in 1871 in Binghamton, N.Y., Charles I. Corby and his brother, William, revolutionized the baking industry. The Corby Brothers moved to Washington, D.C., around 1890 and opened a small bakery. They began growing their business using automation and other baking improvements. The brothers patented a number of their techniques and equipment designs.

"An article in the October 1915 edition of *Baker's Review* marveled at the Corby bakery's high-speed mixers with their automatic counters, the dough slides and six-pocket Duchess dough dividers, the Thomson moulders, the Werner & Ffleiderer rounders," according to the Streets of Washington web site.[18]

By 1912, the Corby Brothers were running the largest bakery in the district, employing 165 people, including sixty bakers. They produced 90,000 loaves of bread and two-and-a-half tons of cakes daily. Deliveries were made by 52 horse-drawn wagons (the bakery had an on-site stable for 96 horses) and eight trucks.[19]

"The self-contained factory had its own power plant, well, and refrigerating plant. It even built, painted, and maintained its own wagons," according to the Streets of Washington.[20]

Charles I. Corby and his wife, Hattie, bought the Strathmore near Bethesda and 99 acres in August 1908.

Corby was a tough businessman, but he was also a philanthropist in the city, donating to worthy causes.

He died from a heart attack while watching a polo match in Florida in 1926.

The Corby Brothers Bakery eventually sold to the Continental Baking Company, the bakers of Wonder Bread.[21]

Corby Brothers baking laboratory in 1922. Courtesy of the Library of Congress.

they are all fixed now," *The Sun* reported.[10]

Once the camp was organized and the men fed, the Marines fell into formation and marched from the camp, past the White House Ellipse, up East Executive Avenue and through the East Gate of the White House around 6:30 p.m.

At the South Portico, President Warren G. Harding, the first lady, Major General John Lejeune, and other distinguished guests watched the Marines pass by as Harding returned the salute the marching Marines gave him.

"Observers declared that this is the first time that troops have passed in review through the White House grounds since the Civil War," the *Marine Corps Gazette* reported.[22]

Gen. Butler was leading the Marines in the review, but as he reached the portico, he left them and took his place with the other observers.

As they marched past, the 134-piece Marine Band (a combining of the Fifth, Sixth, and Tenth Regimental Bands) played "Over There," a popular song written by George M. Cohan in 1917 to galvanize not only troops but a nation preparing to fight in WWI.

*"Over there, over there,*
*Send the word, send the word over there*
*That the Yanks are coming, the Yanks are coming*
*The drums rum-tumming everywhere.*
*So prepare, say a prayer,*
*Send the word, send the word to beware -*
*We'll be over, we're coming over,*
*And we won't come back till it's over, over there."*

"For half an hour the troops marched with the rays of a slow-descending sun glinting from the fixed bayonets. First the marchers came with a quick step the strains of music from the band which had taken its station on the lawn before the portico. Then they broke into double time marching – essentially a moderate jog – down slope to the west gate, filing down West Executive avenue to the Ellipse. As the last marcher went by the band following playing 'The End of a Perfect Day' in tribute to Mrs. Harding," *The Washington Post* reported.[23]

The song (actually "A Perfect Day" by Carrie Jacobs-Bond) was a favorite of the first lady. The final lines also tied up the presidential review nicely.

*"For mem-'ry has painted this perfect day with colors that never fade*
*And we find, at the end of a perfect day, The soul of a friend we've made."*

Gen. Butler was hopeful that the Civil War-related maneuvers would be instrumental in creating a bond of friendship between his Marine Corps and the politicians who had been reading about them and attending the various events. General Butler was fervent in trying to save his beloved Marine Corps, essentially with schmoozing and by continually gaining good, positive press.

The Marines then returned to Potomac Park for another review before acting Secretary of the Navy, Theodore Roosevelt, III, on the southern half of the Ellipse in Potomac Park. Along with Roosevelt were members of the Senate and House of Representatives, dignitaries from foreign governments and high-ranking members of the Army and Navy in attendance. Additionally, thousands of spectators from Washington crowded the roads leading to the park to watch this review.

## Bethesda

Reveille sounded at 4 a.m. and the tired Marines rose from their bedrolls and began disassembling a camp that they had erected little more than half a day earlier. By 6 a.m. on Tuesday morning, June 21, the Marines marched out of Camp Lejeune led by the Expeditionary Force Marine Corps Band.

"Although the hour was early as the force swung out of the Capital, a considerable crowd cheered the marchers as they passed from East Potomac Park to the route leading to Wisconsin Ave,, and out," *The Washington Post* reported.[24]

They headed up Wisconsin Avenue and out of Washington D. C. along roads that had been cleared of traffic by the district police. The thousands of infantrymen marched along at roughly 3 mph while the artillery pieces and tanks traveled about twice that speed. Captain W. S. Shelby, an administrative aid to the District Police, estimated that walking eight abreast, it would take three hours for the Marine line to pass.[25] This was an improvement on the previous day's pace but still slow.

The Marines left East Potomac Park better than they had found it. *The Sun* noted, "the acres where the 5,000 had slept were bare, not only of marines but of their tents, their bread crusts, their waste wood and paper, their cigarette butts, burnt matches and every other sign that they had been there. They left Camp Lejeune cleaner than they had found it."[26]

The day's march was 12.5 miles and stretched out for more than a mile along Rockville Pike. At one point, the line of more than 4,000 marines, 24 guns, and more than 200 trucks was reported to be two miles long.[27] They marched along tree-lined roads, looking out upon fields full of corn, wheat, or grazing cattle.

"Equipped with the most modern and up-to-date war machinery this column of Marine troops will pass through the same villages and over the same roads that marked the Union Army's journey north

# ALFRED C. TOLSON

Albert C. Tolson was 79 years old and one of four known Civil War veterans in Montgomery County, Md., at the time of the Marines' march to Gettysburg.

Tolson joined the Maryland Infantry, First Company B (Confederate) consisting of men from Prince George's and St. Mary's counties. Capt. George Emack of Prince George's County commanded the company.[30]

Tolson actually fought in the Battle of Gettysburg where he was captured by Union troops.

"On the last night of the Battle of Gettysburg he went up in the wake of Pickett's woeful charge bearing chloroform to sooth the wounded who lay out in front. He met the Federals in hot pursuit and was captured," *The (Baltimore) Sun* reported.[31]

He was held prisoner at Point Lookout Prison Camp in Maryland until December 1864 when he was paroled.

Tolson died on April 10, 1928.[32]

to Gettysburg when it kept between the Confederate Army and the National Capitol," the *Marine Corps Gazette* reported.[28]

During the much-shorter march to Fredericksburg in 1921, seven Marines had died. On the first day's march nine men hadn't been able to keep pace.[29] That was not the case this year. Each company had four Cole carts, essentially hand carts, on which they piled the lower roll of their packs, which was the heaviest part of the pack. A pair of Marines pulled each cart for a distance before they switched with another pair. It was a rough time for Marines pulling the cart, but it lasted for only a short stretch of the march. "But by the time the fourth or fifth pair of men take their turn, they are normally tired with marching, and the pulling comes hard. And they say 'The hills are hell,'" *The Sun* reported.[33]

At one point along the march, the Marines heard a bugle blow and then the sound of drums beating. When they looked around for the source of the sounds, they saw it came from a small, vine-covered house. "A boy in a scout uniform stood at the porch rail with a bugle at his lips. Back in the shadows of the vine they caught a glimpse of two people, a man and a woman. The man was white-haired and in his shirt sleeves, and he was rattling a drum with a deft handed roll. The woman sat further back beating the noise out of a big bass drum," according to *The Sun*.[34]

The family was identified as Frank E. Webner and his wife and their son, Gordon. Neighbors said the family had been practicing their performance for the Marines for a week. However, when facing all of the Marines, Gordon became embarrassed when he thought the Marines were making fun of him with all of their pointing and murmuring. He stopped playing and tried to step back in the shadows, but his father pushed him back to the railing.

Marines pose for a photograph while standing in the "chow line" at Camp Lejeune, June 19.

"Play, son, play," Frank told his son.

Gordon obeyed. "His face was as earnest as the face of a Senator saving his country on the floor of the upper House. On the lips of the snowy-haired woman a faint smile played and she walloped the bass drum faithfully every time her husband got a firmer grip on his sticks and resumed the majestic cadences of a march," *The Sun* reported.[35]

The area chosen for the Marines' second night camp was near present-day Garrett Park, a town of 159 people at the time. Some of the residents had electricity, but there was no sewer system. People worried about the invasion of big city ideals. For instance, Sunday baseball games were banned by ordinance on June 10, 1922. For all that worry, the town was indeed invaded and overwhelmed when the Marines arrived.[36]

Maj. Gen. John A. Lejeune reviewed the line along the march. The Marines stopped at the Corby estate just outside of Bethesda at 11 a.m. and began setting up Camp Neville in honor of Maj. Gen. Wendell C. Neville.

Once the camp was set up, local officials and some curious residents toured the camp. "Ralph Donnelly, a boy of nine at that time (11019 Kenilworth, in 1974 the Kornbergs'), remembers the intense excitement of the kids who hung around the camp. Though the Marines were here for only one night enroute to Gettysburg and one night on the way back to Quantico, their visit was a high spot in the lives of the kids of the early Twenties," according to the Garrett Park web site.[37]

That evening the Marines headed over to the east end of the estate that formed a natural amphitheater. The troops enjoyed a cartoon and then watched themselves in Washington, D.C. the day before. The Marine Photographic Section had filmed the Marines and the Navy Aviation Photographic Lab then developed and rushed the film to the Corby estate to be viewed the next day. Chap-

lain Edwin B. Niver took on the duty of bringing the theater along for the Marines and making sure they had evening entertainment.[38]

"It is the first time on record when a force on the march has taken its own moving pictures and seen them exhibited within 24 hours. The show greatly pleased the men and was also viewed by members of the Corby family and several nearby residents," *The Washington Post* reported.[39]

## Gaithersburg

The following day, June 22, the East Coast Expeditionary Force once again got an early start. They broke camp and were on the march by 6 a.m. They headed north on Rockville Pike toward Gaithersburg and their next camp 12 miles away.

As happened with many towns along the route, the residents of Rockville turned out to watch the largest military procession in their lives pass by their homes and businesses. The Marines tried to give them a good show, too, singing as they marched along the roads.

"It seemed that every one was out to see the troops in Rockville. Front porches were filled with people, clerks watched from stores, and business was suspended excepting that was done to serve the men as they took the opportunity to quench their first or replenish the supply of tobacco or cigarettes. Water bottles were filled and many kinds of residents delighted in throwing fruit to the men who rested along the curb," *The Washington Post* reported.[40]

As they marched, perspiring and tired, one of the Marines would call out, "Are we tired?"

"No, we're not!" came the response.[41]

The line of trucks, tractors, wagons and men was said to stretch about five miles along the Rockville Pike through the town.[42]

Rockville Mayor Otis M. Linthicum stood on the public square and welcomed the Marines as

they passed through. Alfred Tolson, a Civil War veteran who now served on the Montgomery County Orphans' Court, was also on hand to watch the parade of Marines from the porch of the Mongtomery House. He had been a dispatch rider in the First Maryland Cavalry.[43]

"I'm afraid we old boys don't make as good a showing as we might," Tolson told the Marines. "There used to be 190 of us, but now there's only four that I know of. I wish they were all here. But Elgar Tschiffely and William Boland, they're off to Richmond, at the Confederate reunion, and John Holland, he lives way up country."[44]

When Gen. Butler found out that Tolson was a Civil War veteran, he anxiously shook the man's hand. Tolson seemed surprised.

"I was on the other side then, general," Tolson told him, admitting that he had served in the Confederate Army with the First Maryland Cavalry.

"There is no other side," Butler told him.[45] "That's all over. You had a lot of good men for comrades," Butler replied.[46]

While the first two days of the expedition had been easy marching, this third day of the march, the Marines would begin their training exercises. The Marines were instructed to send out scouts and proceed as if they were in a hostile environment. The exercise was to assume that a hostile force had captured Gaithersburg and the railhead. It was the Marines' job to free the town and its residents.[47]

"Warily and in scattered detachment, preceded by skirmishers and advance guards who would 'clean out the enemy' in the roadside woods. The 'enemy' had their American flags hanging out and 'sniped' the marines with apples, oranges, drinks of water and bottles of milk," *The Washington Post* reported.[48]

Around noon, the scouts made contact with a supposedly hostile army advancing toward the Marine column. Messages were dropped from the airplanes to Marines on the ground and the Marines

Marine bathes next to "water buffalos," the name for the wagons used in transporting water. Camp Harding, 1922.

# Baths

Though the Marines had plenty of cold water to drink, hot baths were a rarity during the march to Gettysburg and back.

Major Joseph C. Fegan decided during the Marines' stay near Rockville that he needed to get a bath. He was feeling "soiled and creepy." He went into town in search of a bath. He asked the postmaster where he could get one.

"I don't rightly know. You might go down and see Mr. Blank in the next block; I think he has a bathtub. I've heard he has."

So Fegan walked on and found Blank and asked if he had a bathtub.

"Yes, I've got a bathtub, but it ain't in very good shape," Blank said. "I've been meaning to get it fixed up for the last couple years, but I ain't got around to it yet. Sorry, stranger. But you might go see Dr. Blank. He's outside of town a little ways. He's got all kinds of doo-dads on his place."

So Fegan made his way out of town about a mile, feeling dirtier every step of the way. He knocked on the door to the doctor's house and the doctor's daughter answered. Embarassed, he managed to ask about a bath.

"The young lady squared her sho[u]lders, vowed that the women of Montgomery should do their utmost for their country, and directed Major Fegan to the bathroom," *The (Baltimore) Sun* reported.

Soon, Fegan was immersed in a hot bath, scrubbing away two days worth of dirt and crime. The bath lasted for half an hour before he finally climbed out "and in an hour was as dirty as ever again," according to *The Sun*.[50]

reacted as if they were in an actual hostile situation.

"Fighting imaginary foes is the 'Gyrenes' idea of something to do on a quiet evening at home when one is tired of bridge and knitting. The United States marine is not an enthusiastic shadow boxer. He likes to feel a wallop land," according to *The Sun*.[49]

The exercises lasted for about two hours and the Marines finished their march and erected Camp Richards, named for Brigadier General George Richards, in a field of daisies, black-eye susans, and blue bells, about two miles north of Gaithersburg near Seneca Run.[51]

After a shake-down day and two days of marching, the Marines would spend two nights here. Camp Richards had already been set up with a regimental "post exchange" being one of the early tents set up to sell soda, pie, and chocolate to the relaxing Marines. Other improvements that were made in the camp wouldn't be found in other camps along the march except for Gettysburg. These included electric lights and telephones in many of the officers' tents.[52]

In addition to whatever snack food they bought for themselves to eat, the field kitchens were serving one-and-a-quarter tons of food each day to the Marines. "By the time they get up to Little Round Top and vicinity they will have captured and killed more than sixteen tons of vitamins and calories," *The Sun* reported.[53]

They watched the evening's films and some of them walked back to Gaithersburg for some additional entertainment.

"Tonight more acres of Maryland daises are their beds under the stars, two miles beyond Gaithersburg, and the bugle sings them to sleep with memories of groups of Maryland women and children who made today their 'Marine Day,' waiting patiently at the roadside for hours in automobiles draped with flags, and clapping their hands as long as a marine stayed in sight," *The Sun* reported.[54]

The Marines had been marching with little sleep, going to bed late and rising at 4 a.m., but on Thursday morning, June 22, they got to sleep later since they weren't marching. They only had light duties associated with keeping the camp running smoothly and keeping things in order.

Once camp was set up, the Marines spent the afternoon and next day playing baseball games against American Legion teams from Gaithersburg and Ridgeville. News of the games spurred a lot of corps pride as odds were offered on the Marine team that would play. Five to one odds were offered in sums ranging from fifty to a thousand dollars. "Then as the probabilities of takers grew more and more remote, they became willing to bet

*"The men had a real test today, for the road from Ridgeville to Frederick is a succession of ascents and descents. Hill follows hill like bumps in a roller coaster. So to the toiling men in khaki, never too serious even when their feet burn and their backs creak, named the road 'the Permanent Wave'. Yet they made the distance in record time, rolling into camp before noon."*

- The (Baltimore) Sun, June 25, 1922[57]

**Above:** Marines en route to Gettysburg, 1922. This photo had been frequently printed in reverse (facing the wrong direction), but the side on which the soldiers are wearing their equipment and the mileage sign indicate this is the proper orientation. **Below:** Marines pose in front of the pup tents at Camp Neville near Gaithersburg June 20.

$1,000,000 to a kronen that there would be no joy in Gaithersburg tonight," *The Sun* reported.[55]

Gen. Butler threw out the first ball of the game and for a while it appeared that the Marines would win handily against the team from Gaithersburg. The Marines led 8-5 at the beginning of the ninth inning. Then the Gaithersburg team had an incredible rally, winning the game 11-8.[56]

The first casualty of the trip occurred Thursday when a truck ran over a Marine's foot. Another potential casualty was avoided when Marine pilot George Hamilton made a rough but safe landing in his plane upon returning from Quantico.[58]

## Ridgeville

On Friday morning, June 23, the Marines once again were roused at 4 a.m. in order to be on the road at 6 a.m. Their destination was fifteen miles away near Ridgeville in Carroll County, Md. They camped in a field owned by "Straw" Day.[59]

"The country in which the force now lies teems with history. It was in this region that the Braddock expedition traveled on its march to Fort Duquesne in the French and Indian war. During the first invasion of Maryland by the Confederate army in 1863, the Federal troops marched through here to Fredericksburg. During the advance on Gettysburg in June, 1863, a part of the Confederate cavalry, under Gen. J. E. B. Stuart, came through. The army of Gen. Lee returned southward out of the Shenandoah valley in the spring of 1864 through this country," according to *The Washington Post*.[60]

However, rather than sightsee, the Marines were "simulating in every respect wartime conditions with advance guards and scouting parties continually protecting the main column from the attack of enemy forces," according to the *Marine Corps Gazette*.[61]

Not all of the Marines left the camp, though. The truck drivers and engineers helped strike the camp after the Marines had marched off. They numbered about 250, and "Behind them they clean up the camp sites and demolish bridges, dams and roadways they had built. Ahead they build new dams, bridges and roadways to be demolished twenty-four hours later."[62]

At Mount Airy, Md., the Marines were met by another Civil War veteran of the Confederate Army whose name was Albert Maynard. Mayor Archley Molesworth stood in front of the town post office to welcome them to his town.

## Frederick

The Marines left Ridgeville on Saturday morning along the National Pike, heading towards the Frederick City fairgrounds east of the city. *The (Frederick) News* noted that the road conditions along the pike were less than ideal and that the Marines nicknamed it the "roller coaster road" for its many hills.[63]

The march to Frederick was 13 miles and the Marines were given a 10-minute rest out of each hour. "General Butler has introduced an innovation for the infantrymen by relieving them from the heavy packs which they have been accustomed to carry on their backs. These packs are now placed in a cart," *The Frederick Post* reported.[64] The result of having a lighter load to carry meant that the Marines appeared fresher and that there were fewer stragglers.

The first Marines began arriving in Frederick at 9 a.m., but the bulk of the group arrived around noon. By then, streetcars were carrying signs hanging along their sides announcing that the Marines had arrived at the fairgrounds.[65] The Marines were greeted with flags hanging from windows and thou-

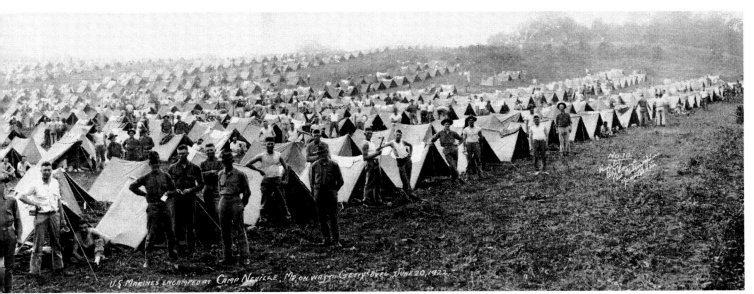

sands of people lining the road into Frederick.

"The old Frederick fair grounds, scene of famous gatherings each fall of people from all over the State to see horse races, prize pigs, pumpkins and side show freaks, is today a city of pup tents and motortrucks, with radio towers rising into the air at one side, smoke curling up from scores of field kitchens and band music floating down toward the city from leatherneck bands. Hundreds of automobiles journeyed out to see the sight," *The Sun* reported.[66]

Once the Marines were encamped, Frederick Mayor Lloyd C. Culler led a delegation out to the fairgrounds to greet the Marines. Besides Culler, the delegation included Lorenzo Mullinix, president of Frederick Board of Aldermen; James H. Gambrill, Jr., Frederick Rotary Club president; Col. D. J. Markey on behalf of the Maryland governor and National Guard; Holmes D. Baker, president of the Frederick Chamber of Commerce; Albert S. Brown representing the Sons of the American Revolution; Rev. William Storm, vice-commander of the Maryland Department of the American Legion; Grayson H. Staley, president of the Frederick Kiwanis Club; David C. Winebrenner and Charles C. Carty.[67]

Culler urged General Butler to stay through Sunday, but Butler insisted there was a schedule that had to be kept. However, Butler did invite any Civil War veterans in Frederick to be special guests of the Marines at Gettysburg.[68] Gen. Butler attended a chamber of commerce dinner in Braddock Heights to the west of the city that evening as their guest of honor.[69]

After the Marines had settled into camp Saturday afternoon, many of them watched the baseball game between the Frederick Hustlers and the Hano-

General Smedley Butler is seen escorting his Marines along North Market Street in Frederick, Md., as they pass through the intersection at East Church Street. The building in the background (52 North Market) still exists, and houses the Candy Kitchen.

Marines march down North Market Street, Frederick, Md., June 24, on their march to Gettysburg.

ver Raiders, which was played on a field right next to the fairgrounds. The teams were part of the class-D professional Blue Ridge Baseball League. The league, which operated throughout most of the 1920s, had teams in Maryland, Pennsylvania, and West Virginia. The Hustlers had won the league championship the previous year, and were leading during the league this season as well.[70]

It wouldn't last, though, and the team would soon start fading. The Saturday game may have been a sign of things to come because Frederick lost 9-7.[71]

That evening the public enjoyed concerts from the Expeditionary Force Marine Corps Band and then later the Marines settled down to watch movies before turning in for the evening.

**Thurmont**

The Sabbath Day saw no rest for the Marines. Once again, they rolled out of their tents, ate breakfast, and readied themselves for the march ahead. This would be the longest hike of the entire march. They would march 18 miles north to reach Thurmont.

Fredericktonians had wanted to see the Marines off, but they hadn't been sure how early the men would be leaving. Some of the residents had gotten up as early as 5 a.m. to line the streets waiting to see the Marines march out of town.[72]

"Gray-hair veterans and the silvery-haired women who had cheered the troops when they came through Maryland to save the North in the days from '61 to '65 watched with sparkling eyes and a far-away reminiscent gaze as they conjured up the scenes of long ago," reported *The Washington Post*.[73]

The Marines marched into the city along East Patrick Street and then headed out of town by going north on Market Street. Though it was very early in the morning, people sat on their porches waving to the Marines as they passed.

"All along the road the Marines have been welcomed by admiring country people who cheer them on and invited them to 'hurry up and come back again and next time stay longer,'" *The Frederick Post* reported.[74]

It was estimated that even with the Marines marching eight abreast, it would still take them three hours to pass any given point.[75]

As the Marines neared the city limits, there had initially been a plan for a Barbara Fritchie reenactor to wave to the Marines as if they were Union

troops in pursuit of Confederates. According to *The Sun*, this didn't happen because Fritchie was considered a controversial topic in the town.

"Though her name is a household word in every Northern household, and millions of Americans know Barbara Frietchie (sic) and her flag defied the Confederate troops, about half of the people of Frederick never mention her name and scoff angrily whenever it comes up," *The Sun* reported.[76]

The woman was already in place at the window, but officials squelched the plan at the last minute.[77]

Besides being the longest hike of the week, June 25 occurred on the hottest day of the march. The heat rippled above the macadam road, reflecting and seemingly baking the Marines.[78]

Another near-accident at the camp revealed that not only were the Marines getting worn out, but so was some of their equipment. Lieutenant Goodyear Kirkman had flown up to the Thurmont campsite early in the morning in one of the Marine airplanes. He had experienced a difficult hard landing on the field and sustained a broken tail skid and air-line to the plane, ruining the carburetor. He needed to return to Frederick, but he had no means of getting there if he didn't fly. He quickly came up with a daring idea.

"He took off from Thurmont controlling his ship with one hand and pumping air with the other, using hand apparatus in place of the broken mechanism. He had to keep pumping furiously all the way. But he made Frederick, landed safely and collapsed from exhaustion," *The Sun* reported.[79]

The Marines had been singing when they left Frederick and they were singing as they entered Thurmont and the last mile of the hike around 1:45 p.m.[80]

"Everyone from the small boy to the aged veteran was up and out to await and see the soldiers. Sunday School and church attendance suffered severely, and no doubt the few who did attend wished they were out on the street. Many persons remained in town preferring to miss their dinners rather than miss seeing this great military outfit arrive. Every porch along the State Road was crowded with people watching the passing trucks," the *Catoctin Clarion* reported.[81]

The Marines ran into a slight snag as they passed north along Church Street. The Western Maryland Railway passed over the road about three blocks north of the downtown square and there wasn't enough clearance for the trucks carrying the tanks to pass under the bridge. Heavy timbers had to be placed on the back of the trucks to allow the tanks to

**Page 42 Top:** Marines relax in Camp Harding awaiting for meals, maneuvers, or tasks to be assigned, 1922. **Page 42 Bottom:** Marines encamped at the Frederick fairgrounds, en route to Gettysburg, 1922.

# AMONG THE MARCHERS

With roughly one quarter of the U.S. Marine Corps on the march to Gettysburg, many of the Marines were heroes who had served in Europe during World War I. "One would think that life with the military outfits that added Belleau Wood and Chateau-Thierry to lists that contain such immortal names as Valley Forge and Gettysburg would teem by night and by day with tales of valor. Yet you seldom hear even the word 'France,' though among the 5,000 are hundreds who fought the whole war through. They simply don't talk about it."[82] Among the Marines on the march were:

- **Captain Le Roy P. Hunt**, Fifth Regiment, won the Distinguished Flying Corss, the Navy Cross, the Croix de Guerre with a palm and a star, and three Army citations. He was wounded at Sois-son during WWI.
- **Sergeant Major W. E. Connolly**, Fifth Regiment, fought in every battle in WWI except the Meuse-Argonne drive. He was wounded during the war.
- **First Sergeant T. M. Haggarity**, Fifth Regiment, was wounded during the war.
- **Sergeant Pat Walsh**, Fifth Regiment, was wounded during the war.
- **Gunnery Sergeant T. G. Bruce**, Fifth Regiment, was wounded during the war.
- **Corporal Thomas Dyer**, Fifth Regiment, was wounded during the war.
- **Gunnery Sergeant Michael T. Finn**, Fifth Regiment, was wounded during the war.
- **Sergeant Charles Strathern**, Sixth Regiment, was wounded three times during the war.
- **Private Eldridge Humphrey**, Sixth Regiment, was wounded at Chateau Thierry and spent 14 months in the hospital only to return and fight at Meuse-Argonne.
- **Gunnery Sergeant Arthur Mattson**, Sixth Regiment, fought in the war but was not wounded.
- **Corporal E. C. Backer**, Sixth Regiment, fought in the war but was not wounded.
- **Private Robert Marendt**, Sixth Regiment, fought in the war but was not wounded.

"... you shall hear how the United States marines are coming deeper into Maryland today, rousing the countryside, bringing the people to their porches, lawns and picket fences, making the advance a veritable march to war past smiling women and children devotedly waving their hands and handkerchiefs, and citizens with serious faces trying to get a meaning out of the columns of lean, strong veterans and youngsters, the trains of guns and the caravans of mighty motors."

– *The Sun*, June 22, 1922[83]

**Above:** Marines entering Thurmont June 25, 1922. **Page 45:** Civil War veterans gather at Thurmont for a group picture.

# Henry C. Fleagle

Henry Clay Fleagle of Thurmont, Md., was the second-to-last Civil War Veteran to die in Frederick County, Md. He was also the last Civil War veteran who was native to the county.

Fleagle died in November 1937 at age 94. He was a first-generation American whose parents had been born in Holland.

He had been born in Unionville, Md., and served in the Civil War under Captain Walter Saunders.

"He served for nearly the entire four-year duration of the war, charging with the line of blue at Gettysburg," the *Catoctin Clarion* reported. He was also at Appomattox Court House when General Robert E. Lee surrendered to General Ulysses S. Grant, ending the Civil War.[84]

The end had been a relief for Fleagle. *The (Frederick) News* reported that he had been only partially conscious the week before his death at the home of his son, George Fleagle.[85]

Henry's wife, Lillie Creager, had died two years earlier. He was survived by one daughter who was married to Wilbur Freeze, four sons, nineteen grandchildren, and twenty great-grandchildren.

Henry was also the last member of the Jason Damuth Post of the Grand Army of the Republic in Thurmont.

Marines moving through Thurmont to Camp Haines on June 25, 1922.

be unloaded. The trucks and tanks then passed under the bridge separately. On the other side, the tanks were loaded onto the trucks again.[86]

By 2:30 p.m., the Marines marched into a clover field about a mile north of Thurmont and sat down. Camp Haines had been erected on the Hooker Lewis Farm for them. *The Sun* reported that thousands of visitors came out to the camp to watch the evening movies with the Marines and listen to the Expeditionary Force Marine Band play.[87] They also joined in singing the Marine Hymn at the end of the concert.[88]

One of the visitors to the camp was Henry Fleagle, a Civil War veteran who fought in 26 major engagements with the Seventh Maryland Infantry and emerged unscathed.

Fleagle saw that the Marines had to carry very little during their march and remarked, "It is hard to get used to the new ways of doing things. We had to carry everything with us when we marched."

"But you didn't have to hike around like this," one Marine told him.

"Didn't, eh? Once we did 30 miles a day, and at the end of it we had to double time three miles to cut off a part of Lee's army, Son, you don't know what hiking is," Fleagle replied.[89]

He told them about fighting in the Battle of Laurel Hill in Virginia during the Civil War when all but four men in his company were killed.[90]

"Once a bullet took my hat away and another time a spent bullet hit me on the shoulder, but it didn't have force enough to go in. I hope you boys will be as lucky as that if there's another war," Fleagle told the gathered Marines.[91]

He shook hands with many of the Marines and officers and told them that were only nine Civil War veterans in the county. Then he thought for a moment, and corrected himself, saying that there may have been only eight left.

By the end of the evening, five other Civil War veterans had visited the camp: Jacob Freeze, "Dad" Elower, Will Miller, William Stull, and Henry Cover.

After eight hours of marching, some of the Marines willingly hiked back into Thurmont after they ate dinner.

"Until late they could be seen walking by the roadside, while many stood on running boards of touring cars whose occupants had honored the uniform and given the sea soldiers desirous of 'seeing the town' a lift to shorten the journey on foot," *The Washington Post* reported.[92]

While in Thurmont, some confusion needed to be sorted out between the Marines and the Commonwealth of Pennsylvania in order for the journey to continue past the Mason-Dixon Line. The Pennsylvania State Highway Department had been told that the Marines were using cleated trucks and tanks that would tear up the road surface. Highway Department officials traveled to Thurmont to inspect the vehicles and make sure that they complied with Pennsylvania law.[93]

As night fell, lights flicked on across the fields breaking up the darkness. Men made their way back to camp before Taps was played. Then they turned in except for officers who worked on the next day's plans and night couriers on motorcycles who carried messages north and south.[94]

## Gettysburg

The next morning, June 26, the Marines made their final fifteen-mile march to Gettysburg, settling in at Camp Harding, near the base of the Virginia Memorial on the Gettysburg battlefield. Once there, they would be able to rest somewhat before returning to Quantico.

The morning started off badly when three Marines were injured near Thurmont. The truck in which they were riding went off the road into a ditch on its way to Emmitsburg. The most-severe injury sustained among the three men was a fractured shoulder blade.[95]

As the Marines passed through Emmitsburg along Seton Avenue, local Civil War veterans—Michael Hoke, Jame T. Hostleborn, John H. Mentzer, Thomas E. Frailey, all of whom had served with the First Maryland Cavalry—stood with flags. Mayor J. Henry Stokes, who had three sons who had served in WWI, also greeted the Marines.

At the state line just north of Emmitsburg, the two Maryland state troopers who had been traveling with the Marines to clear the roads in front of them since they had passed into Maryland from the District of Columbia, turned over their duties to seven Pennsylvania state troopers.[96] The Pennsylvania State Troopers then escorted the East Coast Expeditionary Force on the last leg of their journey on Emmitsburg Road to Camp Harding.

Marines at Camp Haines near Thurmont in 1922. Note the movie screen in the foreground used to show footage filmed while the Marines marching during the previous day.

**Top:** The portable kitchens and tents at Camp Haines in Thurmont. **Bottom:** Several Civil War veterans join the crowd to watch the Marines pass through the Emmitsburg Town Square on the way to the Gettysburg battlefield on June 26. **Page 47:** Cole carts "parked" at Camp Harding in Gettysburg.

# Marines and their baby carriages

During the first day's march from Quantico to Fredericksburg in 1921, nine Marines had fallen out of line and had to be treated for exhaustion from having to haul eighty-seven-pound packs for miles.[97]

In the year following, the Cole cart was introduced to help make it easier for Marines to march further. The cart was originally designed to replace horse-drawn carriages for machine guns, but General Smedley Butler saw that it could also be used to haul other things with relative ease.

"They have been an experiment on this hike. No army on the march has ever before hauled its packs in this way. But the better opinion is that the experiment has established the little carts as a permanent part of marine equipment, and probably of the equipment of the whole blooming *United States Army*. An Army general was out the other day conferring with General Butler about them," *The (Baltimore) Sun* reported.[98]

*The Washington Post* noted that the use of the carts to carry infantry packs "is believed to have placed the marine corps on a more mobile footing, and this is an important consideration with the soldiers of the sea, who frequently receive orders for immediate duty in distant parts of the world."[99]

Dropping the lower rolls of their packs in the hand-cart lightened the load that the Marines were carrying by fifty pounds or more.

Major Edward B. Cole developed the idea for a hand-cart to transport machine guns during World War I. He died in the battle of Belleau Wood shortly after coming up with the idea. He called his idea a pack cart, but Marines often called it a "baby perambulator."[100]

The design is simple. The cart base is a shallow pan attached to a pair of motorcycle tires. A pair of Marines can push or pull the cart by holding onto a pair of long handles.

By piling their packs in the cart, the Marines had much less to carry and could stay fresher. The proof was in the pudding as no Marines dropped out of the march to Gettysburg.[101]

Not all of the Marines were happy with the change, especially if they were the ones pulling the carts. "But by the time the fourth or fifth pair of men take their turn, they are normally tired with marching, and the pulling comes hard. And they say 'The hills are hell,'" *The Sun* reported.[102]

"It is something more than a military camp the marines are putting into the hayfields Pickett charged through. It is a city planned to house and feed nearly 6,000 men and some women."

– The (Baltimore) Sun,
June 28, 1922[1]

# CHAPTER 3

# CAMP HARDING RISES

As the Marines packed up to leave Quantico on their more than 80-mile march to Gettysburg, preparations got under way in Cumberland Township to prepare the historic battlefield of July1-3, 1863, for the planned week and a half long stay of more than 5,000 Marines and local, state, and federal officials and foreign dignitaries.

A area between Emmitsburg Road and West Confederate Avenue, adjacent to Seminary Ridge, was designated as the place for the camp. It was part of the Codori Farm, which at the time, was tenanted by William F. Redding.[2]

*The Gettysburg Times* described the setting thus:

"The country about the camp, much of which is being farmed, presents a beautiful picture with the ripening grain forming huge patches of golden tint, sharply contrasted against the bluish green of the grass fields. The peaceful rural scene, which is so sharply contrasted to the war-like scenes and preparations being made in the Marine Camp, is further carried

**Pages 50-51:** Marines pose to have their pictures taken at Camp Harding, Gettysburg battlefield, 1922. **Page 52:** Camp Harding as it appeared on the Codori Farm in 1922, when it served as home to more than 5,000 Marines from June 26 through July 6, 1922. **Above:** View from behind the High Water Mark looking southwest across the field contested by the Marines in 1922.

out by the appearance of a binder in one of the far off fields of ripened wheat, drawn by four horses, while the farmer seated on it, is clad in blue overalls and wears a large straw hat."[3]

The encampment that would quickly come to be known as Camp Harding, named in honor of President Warren G. Harding. The camp at the Wilderness reenactment in 1921 had also been named Camp Harding. All of the other camps along the marches had been named after Marine generals. By naming the camp after Harding, it not only showed respect for the commander-in-chief, but it also help curry favor from a man whose support was needed to keep the Marine Corps strong.

## The Codori Farm

Camp Harding, from west to east, stretched from West Confederate Avenue to nearly the stone wall that forms a sort of arbitrary boundary on the western slope of the crest of Cemetery Ridge in the immediate vicinity of the legendary High Water Mark.

Before July 1863, the Codori Farm and its accompanying homestead, located in Cumberland Township adjacent to Gettysburg Borough, was the scene of idyllic country life, situated along Emmits-

burg Road, and consisting of generally flat land, perfect for farming.

The most historically significant portion of the farm, relative to the 1922 Marine encampment, lay between Seminary Ridge and Cemetery Ridge, and consisted of relatively flat land rising in a gentle slope eastward from the base of Seminary to the crest of Cemetery.

Standing at the base of Seminary Ridge and looking eastward at Cemetery Ridge across the expanse, the two points seem deceptively closer to one another than they actually are. The distance between the points is roughly 1,000 yards, or a little over half a mile.

Between the eastern base of Seminary Ridge and the western base of Cemetery Ridge, there is little natural cover, aside from slight undulations in the land and wooden fencing at intervals, as the fields sweep eastward towards and across Emmitsburg Road. The only structures that anyone marching across the expanse would have encountered would have been the Codori farmhouse and barn, and some adjacent, associated outbuildings, but those sat on the eastern side of Emmitsburg Road. Along Cemetery Ridge, a stone wall runs roughly north-south along the height of the western side of the ridge.

In the interest of brevity, On July 3, the stone wall across the face of Cemetery Ridge, which essentially fronted on the rear of the Codori property, was occupied by some 6,500 troops from the Union Second Corps, under the command of Major General Winfield S. Hancock, the position bolstered by several batteries along the wall, plus guns on Little

Round Top had enough range to aide in any defense.[4]

More than a half mile away (perhaps as much as three-quarters of a mile away for some of the units involved), lay an estimated 15,000 Confederates, under the overall command of General James Longstreet, who had been placed in charge of the proposed attack by General Robert E. Lee, commander of the Army of Northern Virginia (ANV).[5]

That the assault failed is a matter of historical record, but "historians" have debated for 150 years as to why it did so. All that matters here is that in the wake of it, the failure resulted in the loss of an estimated 3,000 to 4,000 Confederate combatants through death, injury or capture (or absence without leave, a number that the Confederates invariably included among the missing-in-action in their "losses, which the Union Army did not), to about 1,500 casualties suffered by the Union troops opposing the charge, and the ANV withdrew from Pennsylvania, and marched back to Virginia.[6]

Following the battle, more than 500 Confederate soldiers (killed July 2 and 3) were buried on the Codori farm. Pam Newhouse wrote, in *The Codori Family and Farm: In the Path of Battle,* "It should be no surprise that it is believed that more Southern soldiers were buried on Codori property (500 plus) than any other farm on the Battlefield." Most of the dead would eventually be re-interred and returned to their home states for reburial.[7]

### Planning and implementation

Even before units of the Marine East Coast Expeditionary Force left their base of operations at

# "Flyboy" visits college president

On June 21, according to *The Gettysburg Times*, the president of Gettysburg College received a surprise visit from a family friend, who had arrived in a rather unusual manner, landing on the battlefield in the process.

Army aviator Lieutenant Parker Van Sandt (also known as J. Parker Van Sandt), out of Bolling Field, Washington, D.C., was flying north on a military assignment to New York City, when he apparently decided to divert to Gettysburg to see college President Dr. William Granville, and the doctor's wife, Ida Irwin.[8]

Van Sandt had advised the Granvilles in advance to be on the look-out, as he was planning to fly his plane over the president's house June 21, and that he would "fly low over their home three times, so they could identify his machine."[9]

Van Sandt then landed "on the aviation field being laid out for the Marine aeroplanes on the Codori farm."[10]

The lieutenant subsequently applied to the Army for compensation for meals and board while *enroute* to and from New York City, which was tentatively approved in the amount of $41.85, pending the resolution of one of his stays in New York City, for which he could not produce a voucher (the Army contesting an expense of $4.50).[11]

Van Sandt would go on from serving as an officer in the Army Signal Corps during World War I, through establishing his own airline in Arizona, to serving as the deputy secretary of the United States Air Force in the 1940s. He died on June 3, 1990, in a retirement home in Santa Barbara, Ca.[12]

# ATTENDING THE WOUNDED:

The Marine maneuvers and reenactments were already in the planning stage when, in early June, some 200 hospital corpsmen from the Naval Training Station, Hampton Roads, Va., and the Pharmacist's Mates School, Portsmouth, Va., were transferred to Quantico "to fill out the compliment of the medical battalion," naval pharmacist Matthew Birtwistle wrote in 1922.[13] With the more than 80-mile march from Quantico to Gettysburg looming, the medical battalion launched an exercise program to get their medical staff in shape for the long hike, as the "majority were fresh men from civilian life and not seasoned to or familiar with service requirements."[14]

"The coming exercises were to be of a strenuous nature," Birtwistle stated, "and it was early realized that daily drills would be necessary in order to fit the men for the duties required of them. These daily drills on the field at Quantico rounded the men into fine physical condition and stood them well in the severe strain they underwent during the march to Gettysburg."[15]

As did many of the more than 5,000 Marines on the march, the medical corpsmen had to pull along two-man carts containing much of the medical equipment for the journey to the Gettysburg battlefield. But in addition, each evening that the Marine column stopped to encamp for the night, the medical staff had to erect a field hospital to service those who had become exhausted or incapacitated on the day's trek.

The equipment the medical staff had to transport to Gettysburg included: 20 hospital tents; five wall tents; one United States field hospital, 10 folding cots; 10 folding stools; 10 mosquito bars; and one Red Cross flag, not to mention the medical supply chests. Aside from the men on foot, their convoy consisted of four four-wheel-drive trucks, a kitchen trailer, an 800-gallon water trailer (also referred to as a water buffalo), and one motorcycle with a side car.[16]

The medical staff made the task of erecting the hospital tents more manageable by only setting up half of them at each stop, which was deemed sufficient to take care of the day's "casualties." The section erected would remain so until the next section had set theirs up at the next encampment site, at which point the one left behind would break camp and proceed to the new camp. Those Marines who were still being treated as the remaining troops con-

**Above:** The Marine Hospital Corps at Camp Harding: (Top to bottom) Field hospital row; dressing tent; operating tent; and "old campaigners" of the hospital corps. **Page 59:** A Marine offers water to "wounded" compatriot during one of the charges held by the Corps in July 1922.

tinued to march would be shuttled by the ambulance section from the old campsite to the newly established one. "Upon arriving at Gettysburg," Birtwistle wrote, "the sections combined and established the complete field hospital."[17]

The base hospital remained the United States Naval Hospital in Washington, D.C., and Marines who were severely incapacitated during the march were transported to that location for further treatment.[18]

During the Marine reenactments, the Hospital Corps "dressed the wounded and carried them to shelter. "As the troops retreated across the bloody field horse-drawn ambulances went out and gathered in the wounded."[19]

Birtwistle reported that, "to the great credit of these hospital corpsmen who had to hike, not one fell out; and when one stops to consider the physical hardship entailed in the pulling of a medical field chest on wheels over roads for six hours during the month of June, one can not but feel proud of those men who proved their worth and upheld the glory of the Hospital Corps."[20]

Additional medical staff from another branch of the military service arrived at the encampment on June 29. "A demonstration unit of the United States Army Medical Department and attached to the Equipment Laboratory at the Carlisle barracks, arrived in Camp Harding Thursday and have set up camp opposite the Navy Hospital Unit, just west of the Camp Headquarters," *The Gettysburg Times* reported.[21]

The *Times* noted that the Army medical staff brought with them a number of the latest and greatest innovations in field hospitals, including a wagon litter with pneumatic tires, a combat wagon, "which is a great improvement on the old ambulance," a wagon designed especially for the transport of sick or wounded animals, and a field hospital tent with eight windows in each sidewall employing isinglass to allow sunlight to reach the interior during the day.[22]

"On Saturday, they will be joined here by 400 medical men of the Medical Unit, at the Carlisle barracks, many of whom, it is said, will be R.O.T.C. men, who are now taking their yearly training there, " the *Times* stated.[23]

Additional lighting for the hospital set-up was provided by a "unique" truck-mounted generator, which in turn powered "four 75 watt lamps on a stand and using an ordinary tin dish pan for the reflector."[24]

# AIRMAIL SERVICE PROVIDED

Among the services provided to the Marines of Camp Harding during their stay was the establishment of an airmail service for the use of the inhabitants of the encampment.

*The Gettysburg Times* reported, "One of the many unique features about Camp Harding is the manner in which the mail is handled. The mail is handled by the camp authorities and is also received and dispatched by the camp authorities."[25]

Marines were able to, as a result of the arrangement, send and receive letters and other correspondences via a mail plane that was scheduled to pick up and deliver mail at the camp daily, delivering the collected mail to Washington, D.C. and the Marine base at Quantico.[26]

"It has been announced that the mail plane will leave the local camp every afternoon at 4:30 o'clock for Washington and Quantico, with the mail and official reports of the day," the *Times* stated. "Returning, the plane will leave the Quantico headquarters at 9:30 a.m."[27]

Quantico, along with some 1,000 pieces of motorized equipment, including trucks, tractors, tanks, field artillery, and supply and ammunition trucks, work commenced on their temporary home in Cumberland Township on the War Department-owned and managed Gettysburg battlefield.

As early as June 16, *The Gettysburg Times* noted, "A detachment from the Quantico, Virginia barracks are expected to arrive in Gettysburg within a few days to start the operations and have the camp ready for occupancy by the time the main body of troops, under General Smedley D. Butler, arrive here (on June 26)."[28]

But, with less than a dozen days remaining be-

**Above:** 1918 U.S. air mail stamp. **Below:** Marine encampment on the Gettysburg battlefield, June 1922.

fore the proposed camp was to be occupied, some-one among the Marines who had been appointed with planning the encampment, began to question whether or not the proposed encampment would fit onto the land then-allocated.

After assessing the Codori farm site, it was felt by those charged with planning the encampment that the acreage previously allocated on the farm-lands was too undersized to house all the troops, equipment, and other tentage needed to support the more-than-5,000 Marines for the duration of the 10 days they would be encamped. Apparently, planners had neglected to allocate space for the field hospital and related facilities.[29]

The result was that the portion of the site previously earmarked for use by the engineering and signal corps would now have to be reassigned to the field hospital, resulting in the engineering and signal corps being relocated to the eastern edge of the camp "near the Redding farm, where considerable land has been added to the original plot to be occupied by the camp," *The Gettysburg Times* reported.[30]

Also, a result of reconfiguration, the proposed location of the presidential compound, subsequently known as the Canvas White House (Refer to *The Canvas White House* in this chapter.), to be constructed for use of the president and his entourage, also had to be relocated. Although it was not stated where it was to have been initially constructed, the intended footprint was moved to a location along West Confederate Avenue, just north of the North Carolina Monument, and in close proximity to the McMillan farmhouse near the farm and park boundary.[31]

For whatever reason, or due to whatever cause, *The Gettysburg Times* continued to report even up to June 27 that the Canvas White House was being constructed in close proximity to the Virginia monument (also known as the Lee monnument). In their July 3 issue, the newspaper finally had it located in the place where it ultimately existed, in the "extreme northwest corner of the camp."[32]

The ultimate size of the encampment was reported by various newspapers to have been from 65 to 100 acres. Gunnery Sergeant Thomas E. Williams, director of the United States Marine Corps Historical Company, stated that 100 acres is probably closer to the actual size of the encampment.[33]

Another consideration that had to be taken into account, and was considered one of the main priorities of the venture, was the protection of historic battlefield assets, including the land on which they were located. This resulted in a command decision to restrict any heavy vehicles and vehicles hauling heavy loads, to access the camp via Emmitsbug Road, while light vehicles and vehicles carrying lighter loads could travel up West Confederate Avenue.[34]

Among the first teams of Marines who arrived to prepare the encampment site for occupation were members of the First Aviation Group, of which 30 arrived, under the command of Sergeant Crawford, to begin to lay out the space that would be needed for the airplanes for the upcoming maneuvers. Being located on "ground zero" for the upcoming maneuvers, *The Gettysburg Times* even went so far as to note that Crawford and the Marines "arrived in Gettysburg Monday [June 19] ... in two large motor trucks and a touring car."[35]

No doubt that the aviators who arrived early-on were sent with the knowledge that the plotting and construction of airstrips would be needed in advance of all else, since there was an almost immediate demand to establish air transportation to and from the battlefield camp for Marine Corps staff, and for other officials, in order for them to inspect the work as the development of the encampment progressed.

In fact, Marine staff officers, such as Lieutenant Brady, who arrived accompanied by several airplanes on June 19, had likely been compelled to land on one of the airstrip-deficient, vacant fields. Doing so was probably not a problem for the pilots flying the airplanes of the times, who were, no

doubt, rather accustomed to having to land throughout WWI when a prepared landing strip did not always readily present itself as needed. Brady had been sent to allocate the sites for the encampment kitchens, and to help determine the paths of water pipelines.[36]

The battlefield encampment would not serve simply as the temporary home to a handful of airplanes. Some estimates placed the aircraft in service, in respect to the event in one capacity or another, to have been as high as 30. One of the "great mysteries" of the Marines at Gettysburg has been the exact number of aircraft that were involved in some capacity or another at the Gettysburg maneuvers. (See Chapter Four: A tragic beginning: Planes over Gettysburg).

*The Gettysburg Times* reported on June 20, "Twenty-five airplanes, of various types and one captive balloon, will comprise the flying equipment of the airmen, who will be encamped here...while it is expected that some of the officers, attached to this arm of the service will make daily trips back and forth in the flying machines, until the actual encampment is opened."[37]

As the deadline to complete the camp approached, meaning June 26, it became clear the Marines had challenged themselves to a daunting endeavor. "The task has proved so large," *The Gettysburg Times* reported on June 24, "and the time allotted for its accomplishment, so short, that it is said, most of Sunday will be required to complete the work..," also noting that site preparation work was picking up to near frenzy. "The advance detail, sent here has been making rapid progress in laying

out the camp, and erecting temporary structures."[38]

As all of the work progress on the camp proper progressed, much of the fields that would be needed for the maneuvers were covered with ripened wheat waiting to be harvested. Redding, subsequently assisted by another area farmer (who was not identified), began to tackle the task of reaping the standing wheat in the encampment area.[39]

"Beginning tomorrow the United States marines of the famous Fifth and Sixth Regiments will cross the same field, moving as those fighting grandfathers moved 59 years ago; rehearsing for the historical pageant next Monday," the *Baltimore Sun* wrote. "But they already had begun to cross it today, cutting paths with truck trains and motorcycles across the wide plain where minie (*sic*) balls and chain shot swept and men in gray lay down to die."[40]

To facilitate the flow of camp visitors, both dignitary and civilian, "...an information bureau has been established at the main entrance to the camp, from the Emmitsburg Road," *The Gettysburg Times* reported. "There will be men stationed at the Bureau at all times to direct strangers to the various parts of the camp and give other information, which may be sought."[41]

As the night settled on the Marines encamped June 25 at Thurmont, it marked the nearing-end of their trek from Quantico to the Gettysburg battlefield. They would be spending their last night in Maryland, before continuing on the final leg of the march into Pennsylvania and the Gettysburg battlefield on June 26.

But the troops marching, finally, onto the

**Below:** These tank trailers, also called "water buffalo," provided drinking and bath water for the Marines on the road and in the camp. Camp Harding, 1922. **Page 63:** View of one of two of the open-top shower installations erected at Camp Harding for use by the Marines during the 1922 encampment.

"The hot and cold water arrangements were completed this morning, and hard-boiled Marines who have seen the time when they were lucky to be able to break on their morning shaving water, shaved today in luxurious hot suds."
- *The Sun*, June 30, 1922[42]

"hallowed ground" on June 26 found that the work on the encampment and the preparations of the field for battle had not yet been thoroughly completed. Some of the work on the encampment could not, of course, have been completed until they arrived, such as erecting the thousands of tents they had brought with them on the march.

**Infrastructure**

The camp, being more than an aggregation of tents, also needed the infrastructure necessary to support the occupation of the more than 5,000 Marines in the massive encampment, along with numerous U.S and foreign dignitaries, their wives, and various staff members.

As early as June 19, A.B. Plank, a local plumber, who had been awarded the encampment water and sewer contract, began working on water supplies to ensure that the 300 shower baths being installed in two bathhouses, also under construction, received an adequate supply of water. In the end installing all of the water supply infrastructure entailed tapping into the Gettysburg Borough water supply and laying "many miles of pipe line."[43]

The two "bathhouses" would essentially be two wooden-floored, open-air canvas enclosures with the bathroom equipage contained within, one such enclosure being 164 feet by 24 feet, and the second being 140 feet by 12 feet.[44]

On June 27, the Signal Corps was able to establish radio contact with Washington, New York, and Philadelphia, besides the Marine Corps barracks at Quantico, and set up a radio network throughout the encampment to allow officers and staff to communicate with each other on-site, as well as to communicate with the various aircraft when aloft.[45]

*The Gettysburg Times* noted that the connections with Quantico did more than allow radio communications between the camp on the Gettysburg battlefield and their Virginia headquarters. "The feat established a new record for speed in long distance radio communication, as the points were reached within a half hour after the work of establishing the large system...had been started."[46]

The Marines at work on-site also provided the encampment with its own phone service set-up for the troops and their command, with lines also being connected to those of the Bell Telephone company to enable "outside" calls. The phone system thus installed also conceivably made it possible for the encampment to have its own unique telephone exchange.[47]

*The Sun* reported that, by the time the maneuvers began on June 27, "Capt. E.E. Eiler's Signal Corps men had strung nine miles of telephone wire through the old bullet-riddled trees and across the hallowed hayfields and installed about 70 telephones."[48]

*The Gettysburg Times* noted "Even though the full brigade did not reach the camp until late in the afternoon, darkness found electric lights and telephones in the tents of scores of officers. This work was done by the signal outfit"[49]

The men were generally exhausted, so what work remained for them to do regarding the site preparations, other than erecting their own tents, was held off until the next day.

"They worked like beavers, getting the camp into shape not only for themselves but for hundreds of distinguished visitors, including President Harding..." *The Sun* reported on June 27. "Work went on as usual, truck trains beating roadways across the plateau where General Pickett led his men, tents going up, wires being strung, plumbing being put in and chow being cooked."[50]

## The "Canvas White House"

Due to the planned stay of President Harding and his wife, Florence, in the Marine encampment for a portion of the military demonstrations and reenactments at Gettysburg, it was decided to erect a structure for the couple, as well as for use by members of the presidential entourage.

The site chosen was a relatively high point of

> "The Battle of Gettysburg, 1922, will be a hard battle for President Harding. He will have to eat his meals out-of-doors. Except for that he will be almost as comfortable in the midst of this 'war' as though he were at home on Pennsylvania avenue. A little more comfortable, perhaps. He will not have to go upstairs to bed. They have many modern improvements in the Marine Corps, but they haven't yet made tents with second stories."
>
> – *The Baltimore Sun*, July 1, 1922[51]

the field located along West Confederate Avenue, just north of the North Carolina Monument, and was situated in close proximity to the McMillan farmhouse near the farm and park boundary.

The purpose of creating what many referred to as the Canvas White House (also the Gettysburg White House) wasn't merely just to provide a showpiece for the event nor to serve solely as convenient quarters for the president and dignitaries at the maneuvers, though it certainly was all those things as well. The *Sun* reported, "It will house the President and Mrs. Harding...(and) the office force he brings along to keep the executive department of the Government going... so that the country may progress as rapidly, while 'Pickett's Marines' are charging as it does in Washington."[52]

*The Gettysburg Times* described the presidential compound as "one of the most elaborate quarters ever provided the President of the United States in any camp..." *The Sun* compared the appearance of the canvas presidential complex at the encampment site to "a magic castle in the wilderness."[53]

The complex was essentially a "pre-fab (prefabricated)" complex of structures, which was initially designed and constructed at Quantico by Marine Corps mechanics. After the structures comprising the complex were completely assembled at the Marine base, they were then disassembled for shipment and conveyed to the Gettysburg battlefield on-board a number of freight cars, *The Gettysburg Times* reported on June 28.[54]

The newspaper had initially reported on June 24 and June 27 that the disassembled Canvas White House was being transported in trucks, along with the troops the march.[55]

The entire complex of tentage which comprised the presidential compound formed a semi-circle, fronting on a semi-circular drive, as can be seen from aerial photographs taken at the time.

The completed, canvas and wood, nine-

**Page 64:** Interior photograph of the Canvas White House, 1922, Gettysburg Battlefield, by Underwood & Underwood. **Below:** The Canvas White House at it appeared without the additional tentage for male and female guests.

# Sorting it out: Where was the

**Figure 1.** Modified from a base photograph courtesy of the U.S. Marine Corps Historical Company.

Although the presidential compound, referred to as the Canvas White House, was initially planned to be in the area of the Virginia Monument on West Confederate Avenue. It was subsequently relocated to the northwestern portion of the encampment site, north of the North Carolina Monument.[57]

*But exactly where?*

To determine this, the co-authors compared an aerial photograph taken during the June 26-July 4 maneuvers which depicted the Canvas White House (Figure 1).

In Figure 1, the presidential compound (A), a semi-circular arrangement of tentage located at the northwestern corner of the site, can be seen at the lower right. The North Carolina Monument is located at B, while an outstanding tree-lined ravine is located at C, and a fence line that may have demarked the terminus of the Codori Farm adjacent to the McMillan Farm, is located at D.

# Canvas White House?

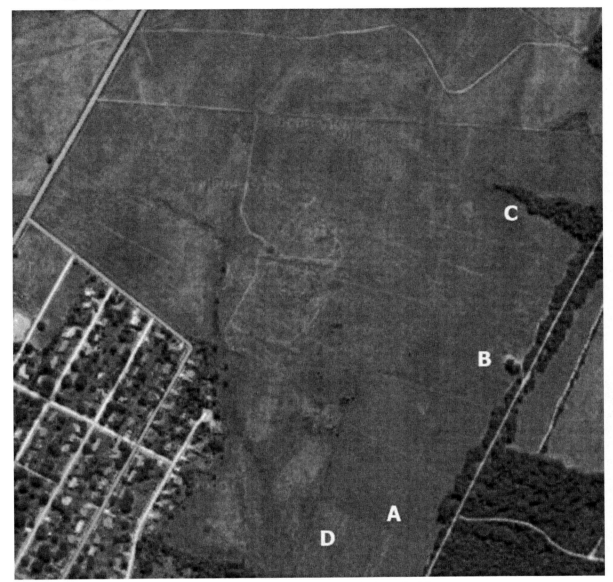

**Figure 2.** Modified from a base photograph courtesy of Google Maps.

The smoke, which appears to have been generated by artillery and signal guns, could have occurred at any time from June 27 to July 4, as the Marines held battle maneuvers on almost every day of the encampment except June 26, the day they arrived, and July 3, when they were given the day off. However, the presidential compound having obviously been completed when the photograph was made, would suggest the photograph was made sometime between June 29 and July 4.

Figure 2 shows a comparable satellite view of the area in Figure 1, with matching areas marked with the appropriate letters. The road to the right off West Confederate Avenue, which would have been behind the compound, did not exist in 1922.

THE WHITE HOUSE
WASHINGTON

# The Canvas White House

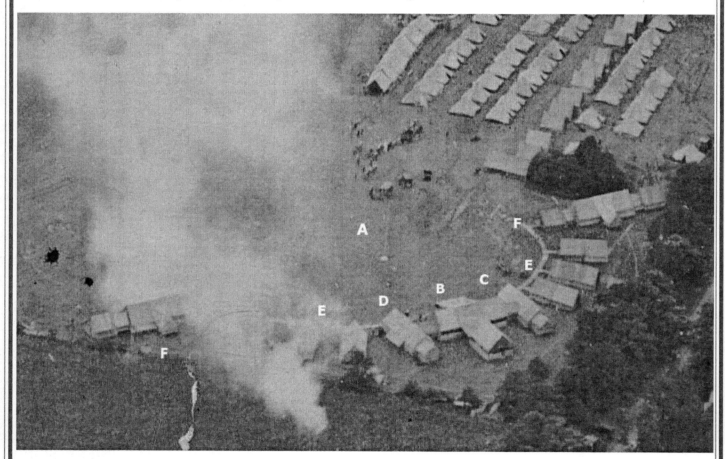

A - The presidential compound
B - President's public reception room
C - President and First Lady Hardings' quarters
D - Presidential Secretary George Christian's quarters
E – Three tents on each side of main tentage for male guests
F – One tent on each side of the compound for female guests[58]

structure complex was 400 feet in length and 175 feet in width, and comprised of 16 rooms (distributed among nine structures that comprised the presidential compound). Initially, the finished compound was to have been painted white, but that plan was amended sometime going into June 29.[56]

*The Gettysburg Times* reported, on June 30 "...it has been decided not to paint the structure white, as originally planned, for it is feared that the paint would not be dry before the President arrives. The exterior effect of the mansion has therefore been changed by using khaki-colored canvas over siding boards, which makes the structure have the appearance of a huge Marine tent."[59]

Additionally, *The Sun*'s account did not agree with that of *The Gettysburg Times* when it came to the number of rooms in the Canvas White House compound. *The Sun* stated, "It will have 24 rooms and six bathrooms..." Of course, the difference in reporting could have been the result in what one might count as constituting a room.[60]

The complex was described as a blend of tent and cottage, which utilized canvas, wires, and wooden siding, and with canvas roofing from hospital, storage, and wall tents. All of the structures were provided with wooden flooring, with a plank walkway constructed along the front of the tents in the compound.[61]

*The Gettysburg Times* also provided a very detailed description of the finished project:

"The floor plan of the large structure is of a unique design, being semi-circular in shape...In the center of the building is the President's public reception room, which is 40 feet in length by 25 feet in width...on either side of the public reception room are large rooms to be used as combination sitting rooms and bed rooms, the one, on the left...being allocated to the president and his wife, while the one on the right will be used by (presidential) Secretary George Christian...In the rear of each of these rooms are private baths, completely finished with all the fittings of a modern bath and the added convenience of hot and cold water."[62]

Three buildings flanked each side of the main presidential setup, each a combination of reception area and bedroom, and were intended to be occupied by the males in the presidential entourage. At the end of each row of three were a larger structure,

Smoke, probably from artillery, wells up behind the Canvas White House

69

each with living-rooms and bedrooms, which were intended to be occupied by the ladies in the presidential group.[63]

The interior walls and ceilings of the Canvas White House were covered with plasterboard and other materials, mainly to conceal certain structural elements, such as otherwise bare studs and rafters.[64]

The presidential compound was also well-lit, with the electricity provided by on-site generators. The generators not only provided enough power for the interior lighting that had been installed in the two-dozen rooms of the complex, but also for "long lines of incandescent bulbs" outside along the frontage of the compound tents.[65]

The Canvas White House was "officially" completed on June 29 with the installation of six porcelain bathtubs, which had been flown in "strapped to" Martin MBT twin-engine bomber/torpedo planes and "flown over the mountains to Gettysburg," *The Sun* reported, noting that there had been a concern the heavy porcelain bathtubs could be damaged during overland transport. "These are the first bathtubs ever carried by airplane, it is believed."[66]

Just for the record, Clayton Barrow, Jr., in an article entitled *Looking for John A. Lejeune,* states, "A photograph taken at Gettysburg shows President Harding's bathtub lashed to the bottom of an airplane. In his caption, Jack (*Editor's Note: Captain John H. "Jack" Craige*) pointed out that the Corps

would spare no expense to ensure the comfort of its Commander in Chief. The tub was indeed the President's, but it had arrived by truck." Unfortunately, Barrow, Jr. apparently did not leave behind a bibliography attached to the article upon which to "stake his claim."[67]

Regarding the furniture for the presidential compound, *The Gettysburg Times* stated that, on Monday, June 26, a "(railroad) carload of interior fixings was unloaded on the switch (railroad siding), near the camp, and stored in a tent there. For the reception rooms in the presidential suite, comfortable wicker furniture in an ivory finish with rich upholstering, has been chosen, while in other reception rooms, massive tapestry furniture will be used. The bedroom furniture is mahogany, in a plain design."[68]

The president, first lady, and the presidential entourage would be sharing their meals in the encampment beneath canvas with other Marines. Noting this, *The Sun* reported, "...the President of the United States will have to 'rough it' in camp with the men who lived on cold, 'canned horse' at Chateau-Thierry (*Editor's Note: The WWI Battle of Château-Thierry was fought on July 18, 1918*)."[69]

**Let the show begin**

Because the maneuvers and reenactments were

**Above:** Marine gets a haircut during the 1922 encampment at Camp Harding. **Below:** Marine trucks, presumably with the Marine Transportation Corps, helped haul heavier loads to the encampment. Notice the Pennsylvania Memorial on the horizon at right center top.

intended to promote the Marine Corps as a whole in the public eye, promotion of the then-upcoming march and public military activities were as much of a necessity to the drawing attention to the Marines, as the event itself.

The Marine Corps had already held one combination field exercise and Civil War reenactment, it being the intent of the organization to hold at least one-a-year, but none would attain the fame of the Gettysburg battlefield event.

Tens of thousands were expected to attend the public events and tour the encampment, but to ensure that the maneuvers would be well-received by the public, the "promoters" would come to rely on major newspapers, newsreel coverage, and help from railroad officials.

First and foremost, those who worked on the promotions turned to whatever newspapers they felt could garner the greatest interest among their respective readerships, and this would fall into the hands of the Gettysburg and Chambersburg chambers of commerce.

The duo of local chambers of commerce would turn to professional help in this regard, and contracted with "an Atlantic City advertising agency, C.W. Rosevear, to publicize the upcoming July activities. C.W. Rosevear was charged with publicizing the Marine event on the historic Gettysburg battlefield throughout much of the country, notably in the newspapers located in the major cities in East and Mid-West, including Baltimore, Washington, Pittsburgh, Cleveland, Chicago, and New York.[70]

Specifically targeted by the chambers via Rosevear were the Sunday editions of seven major newspapers, along with graphics illustrating Pickett's Charge as it had appeared on July 3, 1863, and a recreation of what the planned Fourth of July Marine attack would look like when the Corps would reenact the charge using "modern" technology, such as fighter planes, howitzers and tanks, to name but a few.[71]

Although the time frame for the advertisement was not stated all that clearly in the source materials, it appears the chambers wanted the advertisements to run on June 18. All of the newspapers contacted were apparently agreeable to this, except for the *Chicago Tribune* who reported that, for whatever reason, they could not run it until the Sunday after the targeted one (presumably June 25).[72]

The fact that the advertisements had a significant impact on the attendance during the July through July 4 public demonstrations can be little doubted. "The camp of the Marines has been widely advertised," the *Gettysburg Compiler* wrote, "and large crowds are expected to come here during the dates of the reproduction of Pickett's charge."[73]

The Philadelphia and Reading Railroad also jumped on the bandwagon to promote the event, especially since, no doubt, they would profit from the conveyance of potential attendees.

Local Philadelphia and Reading Railroad agent N.B. Schnurman (occasionally also spelled Schnurmann in some editions of *The Gettysburg Times*) told *The Gettysburg Times* that the railroad "is engaged in an extensive advertising campaign over all lines of the company featuring the events here on July 3 and July 4, together with a general program

Possible members of the Marine Band practice on their instruments in Camp Harding, 1922.

of the Marines encampment in Gettysburg," *The Gettysburg Times* recorded.[74]

However, the newspaper noted on June 17 that the railroad would not be adding-on any special trains to transport tourists to the events, but would simply add-on extra coaches to their regular runs.[75]

The train line would subsequently change their minds regarding this some five days later, when they decided to operate a "one-day excursion" out of Reading on July 2. Obviously, the railroad had come to realize a profit was to be made beyond simply adding-on extra cars on the regular runs for the event, as they had previously indicated four days earlier.[76]

Certainly a major assistance in promoting the affair came in the form of the Pathe Weekly, a major producer and distributor of newsreels at the time, two cameramen of which arrived at Camp Harding on the morning of June 28. As a result, *The Gettysburg Times* noted, "That events at Camp Harding will be broadcasted further than through the newspapers is certain with the arrival of.. (the) two cameramen..."[77]

"Arrangements were being made to take the photographers on a tour over the field in an airplane," *The Gettysburg Times* wrote, "after which they engaged in making feature pictures of the camp, and its surroundings, to be released for showing in the moving picture houses throughout the country on Friday (June 30)."[78]

The making of "moving pictures" on the "field of battle" did not come without a cost, though. *The Sun* reported that a Private B.R. Davis, of the Marine Fifth Regiment, was injured while setting off a bag of black powder that had been used to simulate explosions, when requested by "moving picture men." The newspaper stated, "They placed their cameras, prepared to grind, and Davis ignited the powder bag. But it went off too soon and the camera men got a picture of a soldier at the heart of the flame-burst and a cloud of white smoke. Davis fell, badly burned on the face and hands." The film company involved was not identified in the coverage.[79]

A second individual, Corporal E.L. Blowers,

TOURS.            TOURS.

A Double Incentive to

Visit Gettysburg Battlefield

Its Historical interest and

United States Marine Encampment
June 26th to July 6th

6,000 Marines with a squadron of Aeroplanes
These will all participate in a

REPRODUCTION OF PICKETT'S
FAMOUS CHARGE ON JULY 3rd
Followed by
THE PICKETT CHARGE UNDER CONDITIONS OF
MODERN WARFARE ON JULY 4TH
When leading civil and military men of the nation will be present
Ample Hotel and Garage Accommodations.
TRAVEL on "The Main Street of America,"

THE LINCOLN HIGHWAY

For complete details of program and information regarding auto
routes, etc. address Secretary, Chamber of Commerce, Gettysburg, Pa.
or Secretary, Chamber of Commerce, Chambersburg, Pa.

was also injured in a similar manner. The *Sun* reported that the corporal's incident did not occur in conjunction with the film production. *The Washington Times* reported that it did.[80]

As late into the maneuvers as June 30, *The Sun* noted, "D.E. Griffith, the motion picture director, has promised to 'join the marines' in Gettysburg before President Harding comes, to lend the help of an expert stage manager to the spectacle of the marines' own battle of Gettysburg."[81]

The success of the promotional effort was reflected in the tens of thousands of spectators who came to witness the publicly-held military maneuvers and touring the Marine camp, although the estimated crowds varies from newspaper to newspaper, numbers that would unlikely be seen again in and around Gettysburg until the advent of the modern reenactments that would follow decades later.

Craige summed up the effect of the overall promotional effort in his September 1922 article, "The Marines at Gettysburg," in the *Marine Corps Gazette*: "In the field of attracting the favorable notice of the Nation to the activities of the Marine Corps, equal success was achieved. Several thousand columns of newspaper clippings have been received at Headquarters, cut from the papers of cities all over the country, from Maine to California, and articles in magazines are still making their appearance, dealing with phases of the march and the exercises at Gettysburg. On the day following the President's visit to Camp Hording at Gettysburg, newspapers all over the country carried frontpage stories of the demonstration in his honor and, thereafter, illustrated pages, rotogravure sections, illustrated magazines and the like were filled with pictures of the doings of the Marines, while moving pictures of the exercises appeared on the program of every one of the great weekly moving-picture concerns."[82]

"It is probable that future war will be conducted by a special class...as it was by the armored Knights of the Middle Ages."

— *Brigadier General William 'Billy' Mitchell,*
*"Winged Defense," 1924*[1]

Aviation Section
U.S.M.C. G.F.
Oct 1921 By 1918

# CHAPTER 4

# KNIGHTS OF THE AIR

The column of Marines, along with the equipment that accompanied them, had successfully trekked some 80 miles, marching from Quanitico, Virginia, to Washington, D.C., into suburban and rural Maryland, and finally across the Mason-Dixon Line into Pennsylvania, arriving in Cumberland Township, the location of their immense encampment on June 26, and site of the July 3, 1863, battle that came to be known as Pickett's Charge.

All along the route of the march of the Marines from start-to-finish, the Marine First Aviation Group provided "simulated" air protection in their fighters and their scout planes for the column as it advanced. Most of the Marines, and certainly the media, admitted, the "fly boys" — these "knights of the air," as they were frequently labeled in World War I — were stealing the show along the line-of-march, and would especially do so with their simu-

lated aerial attacks over the battlefield during the upcoming Pickett's Charge reenactments.

But air combat, in times of war, and in simulations even in times of peace, often did not come without a price. In the seemingly fragile wood and canvas airplanes of the 1910s and 1920s, when things went wrong, it not infrequently went very, very wrong.

## Planes over Gettysburg

As part of the week-long training and military demonstrations to be held on the Gettysburg battlefield, much of the Marine First Aviation Group was dispatched to Camp Harding to participate, including de Havilland DH-4Bs, which served as a light bomber, fighter, and observation craft, Vought VE-7 training and observation planes, Martin MBT bomber/torpedo planes, and two Type-F kite observation balloons.[2]

All of these planes were of the bi-wing type, meaning they possessed upper and lower sets of wings. The kite balloons were inflated with highly-explosive hydrogen, and were tethered to the ground via cables (thus the term kite). They were also called "captive" balloons, meaning they were connected to the ground and not free-flying, maneuverable crafts.

The DH-4B, which had evolved after the end of WWI from the more infamous DH4, served the Marines as its primary fighter going into 1922. The WWI DH4 was responsible for the entire de Havil-

**Pages 74-75:** Parked Marine aircraft at Brown Field, Quantico, 1922. From left to right: five de Havilland dive bombers; Vought trainer/observation plane; Martin MBT bomber/torpedo plane. These may well have been among the planes in Gettysburg for the June-July maneuvers. **Page 76:** Dive bombers, observation, and bomber/torpedo planes of the U.S. Marine First Aviation Group parked on the Gettysburg battlefield during the 1922 maneuvers. Rear row (facing camera): Martin MBT bomber/torpedo planes. Middle and Front row (from left to right) each contain: One Vought VE-7 training/observation plane and two de Havilland DH-4Bs. **Above:** De Havilland dive bombers flying over Marine Flying Field, Miami, in 1918.

# "Devil Dogs" with Wings

Marine mascot Sergeant Major Jiggs poses in the cockpit of a Marine dive bomber. Jiggs was purchased for the Marines by General Smedley Butler in 1921. The bull dog died in 1927, and was buried at Quantico with full military

The Marines were essentially established as the Navy's infantry force (eventually leading to the Marines also being referred to as the "sea soldiers"), tracing their lineage back to the American Revolution, having been created by a resolution of the Continental Congress on November 10, 1775, with Samuel Nicholas having been designated their first commander.[3]

The Marines fought in virtually all of the major wars entered into by the United States to date, as well as a host of small military confrontations in various ports-of-call, but the Corps' first severe and most brutal baptism by fire was almost certainly World War I.

A host of members of the Marines garnered the nation's highest awards in the conflict, many

of whom would participate in the 1922 maneuvers and reenactments on the Gettysburg battlefield – one of whom even dying there.

But one of the outcomes of that "war to end all wars" would lead to the establishment of the Marine aviators, an effort credited to then-Lieutenant Alfred A. Cunningham, who, during that war, ultimately acted as the de facto director of what then existed of Marine aviation.[4]

The long and winding road of creating the Marine First Aviation Group, which is the main subject of this chapter, would not be warranted herein in detail, and will simply be outlined thus:

Evolution of the Marine First Aviation Group:[5]

From the moment a Marine aviator climbed into a cockpit during WWI, a struggle ensued to establish an identity for Marine aviation. During much of 1917, the Marine aviator organizations initially concentrated primarily on seaplanes assigned to anti-submarine sorties:[6]

- Establishment of the Marine Corps Reserve Flying Corps authorized.
- Up to circa 1916: Marine Section of the Naval Flying School (aka Aviation Section);
- 1917: Formation of the Marine Corps Aviation Company;
- 1917: Marine Corps Aviation Company renamed Marine Aeronautic Company.

By mid-year 1917, efforts were made to create a land-based Marine air force to support ground troops:[21]

- Late-1917: Formation of the First Aeronautic Company (for seaplane duty), the First Aviation Squadron (for land troops support and operations), and the Aeronautic Detachment;
- 1918: Formation of the First Marine Aviation Force.

In 1922, all of the Marine aviation units which had come to be based out of Quantico were redesignated the Marines First Aviation Group, with three primary squadrons, one for combat aircraft, one for observation aircraft, and one for balloons, just in time, so to speak, for the "air wars" above Gettysburg.

*Editor's Note: Marines became known as the Devil Dogs as the result of a name reportedly given to them by their German enemies during the Battle of Belleau Wood toward the end of WWI. ("Belleau Wood." 6thmarines.marines.mil. Accessed January 1, 2015.)*

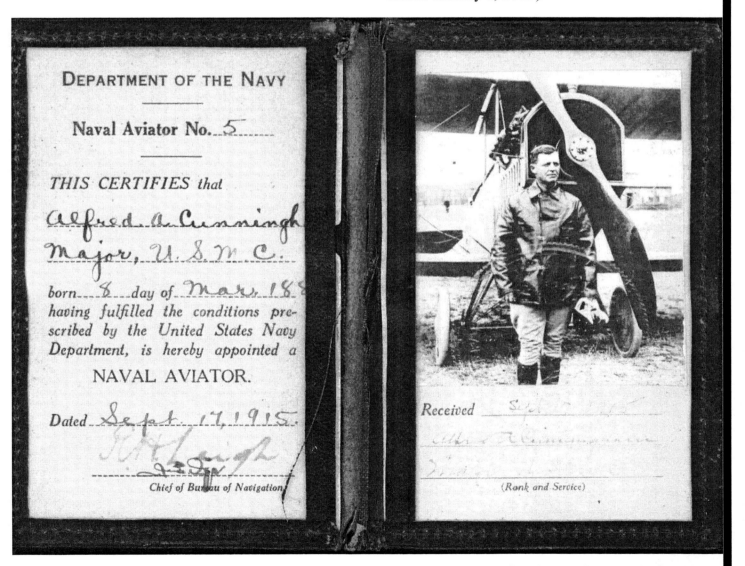

Naval Aviator Certificate issued to Navy Lieutenant Alfred A. Cunningham in 1915. Cunningham became the first Marine aviator, and, in the wake of World War I, was made officer-in-charge of Marine Corps aviation.

land DH series having been dubbed "flaming coffins (also called "flying coffins")," because, according to the National Museum of the U.S. Air Force, "the pressurized gas tank had a tendency to explode and a rubber fuel line under the exhaust manifold caused some fires." Even more, "the location of the gas tank between the pilot and observer limited communication and could crush the pilot in an accident."[7]

Fortunately, and especially for those ultimately employed in simulated aerial combat at various Marine maneuvers and public Civil War reenactments, the DH4 underwent modifications between 1919 and 1923 which eliminated major safety concerns, and involved "moving the pilot's seat back and the now unpressurized gas tank forward," and "skinning the entire fuselage with plywood." The modified planes were designated DH-4B.[8]

The DH-4B was armed with two forward-firing 30-caliber machine guns and two 30-caliber machine guns at the rear cockpit. The plane was also capable of carrying up to 322 pounds of bombs on its wings.[9]

The VE-7, produced by Lewis & Vought at the end of WWI, served primarily as a two-seat, "advanced trainer" and as a "tug" (to pull gliders

**Above:** Two DH-4Bs (left) and two VE-7s (right) can been seen parked in the background of the Camp Harding encampment photograph. **Page 81 Top:** The Martin MB (specifically an MB-1) bomber was the type bomber which spawned the Martin MBT (and other variants), this one photographed as it flew over Washington, D.C. The bomber was later "pacified" to carry mail for the early U.S. air mail service. **Page 81 Bottom:** The Martin MBT was a bomber (MB) that had also been modified to carry torpedoes (thus the MBT designation). The Marine sent three of these to participate in the 1922 Gettysburg battlefield maneuvers. They were also used to haul heavy freight, including the bathtubs for the presidential compound in Camp Harding. Photographed at an unknown location.

# Sorting it out:
# Where was the First Aviation Group?

Members of the Marine First Aviation Group began laying-out air strips early on as Camp Harding started taking shape.

One of the reasons for the jump-start on establishing the landing areas was to facilitate shunting staff back-and-forth from Washington and Quantico who were involved in various aspects of bringing the paper plans for Camp Harding to life.

Figure 1: Figure 1 depicts the aviation area (B) as being northeast of the Virginia Monument (A). But a better "pointer" can be found in Figure 2, in which the tree-lined ravine (A) just south of the North Carolina monument points directly in the direction of the air field (B). The road at the top of the photo is not Emmitsbrg Road. This was a road constructed just west of Emmitsburg Road within the boundaries of the encampment.

Figure 2: Using the two figures, it can be seen that the airfield was located at (A) in Figure 3. Emmitsburg Road cuts across the lower right-hand corner and intersections with Long Lane two-thirds up the right side.

Figure 3.

The de Havilland DH4B dive bomber was one of the mainstays of post-WWI Marine aviation through the 1920s.

and targets), although it served a brief time as a designated fighter, and was occasionally used for scouting and observation. The VE-7 was generally an unarmed plane, although some variations were armed with one or two Vickers or Browning machine guns.[10]

Of the three plane types at the event, the big, twin engine Martin MBT bomber/torpedo planes seemed to garner the attention of most of the media, and likely, most of the tourists. The Martin MBT was manufactured by the Glenn L. Martin Company beginning in 1920. The planes spanned just over 74 feet from wing tip to wing tip, and 42 feet in length. The plane with armed with two 30-caliber machine guns in the nose and two 30-caliber machine guns in the rear cockpit, and was capable of carrying a 1,618- pound torpedo under the fuselage.[11]

The actual numbers of each of the aircraft types sent to the Gettysburg battlefield encampment seem to vary to some degree, depending on which account one refers to, although most generally agree that there were three Martin bombers and the two observation balloons (there are sources that only mention one balloon). However, the participating DH-4B fighter planes have been given from five to six, and the numbers of Vought VE-7 planes have ranged from six to eight.

Some photographs of the encampment show two observation balloons aloft at the same time,

and another photograph shows three Martins side -by-side on the ground in the camp, but different photographs show a different array of DH-4Bs and VE-7s parked in the air section. However, since at least two are aerial photographs taken from one or more of the aircraft, it is impossible to know what mix or how many were in the air at the time the pictures were taken, or on other assignments. It is known, for example, that there were one, and probably several, dedicated to air mail service between the encampment site, Washington, D.C, and Quantico at the time.[12]

The "The Aircraft Squadrons" stated there were six DH-4B and six VE-7, while it is reported in the July 1922 *Leatherneck Magazine* there were seven DH-4B and eight VE-7, but does mention there were 18 in action, which would add up if the three Martin bombers were included.[13]

Mark Mortensen, in his book *George W. Hamilton, USMC: America's Greatest World War I Hero*, wrote that "Thirty planes were scheduled to assist the ground troops in the mock battle," while *Leatherneck Magazine*, in the same article that gave the numbers of types that added-up to 18, also stated, "operations were conducted from there with twenty planes of different types." That difference could be explained by the coming-and-going of flights ferrying supplies and passengers between Quantico and Camp Harding involving planes that

Although the Vought VE-7, such as the one shown, was intended as a training plane, it was briefly designated a fighter, and also served as a scout and for observation.

were not directly involved in the maneuvers. The Marine air force did possess an array of other airplane types, which would explain the "twenty different planes" noted in *Leatherneck Magazine*.[14]

That there were more planes involved in the overall effort beyond those involved in the actual reenactments was also reinforced by an article in *The Washington Post*, which stated, "...more than 30 planes will be with the force for distribution among various units."[15]

The most-reliable source would seem to be the numbers offered in the 1922 *United States Air Services* journal, which states 17 "active Marine Corps pilots" participated, and specifically identifies them. Further, the publication states there were 20 planes, including seven DH-4Bs, eight VE-7s and three Martins, which, of course, doesn't add-up to 20, unless "planes" should have read "aircraft," since the additional two observation balloons would have made 20 aircraft.[16]

Pilots who participated in the actual combat exercises were identified as: Major Roy S. Geiger; captains Louis M. Bourne, Jr.; James E. Davis; James T. Moore; and Francis P. Mulcahy; first lieutenants John B. Bates; Harold D. Campbell; Walter G. Farrell; Basil G. Bradley; and William J. Wallace; and second lieutenants Goodyear W. Kirkman; Leo Sullivan; Hayne D. Boyden; James K. Noble; Earl F. Ward; Wallace D. Culbertson; and Benjamin Reisweber.[17]

But the reader will notice that 18 airplanes are given (seven DH-4B, eight VE-7 and three Martins), but only 17 pilots who "took part in the exer-

cises" are named. That can easily be explained by the fact that the eighteenth pilot was killed while attempting to land on arrival at the Gettysburg battlefield encampment, and thus did not participate, although his plane was likely still counted as having been there.[18]

The one pilot not mentioned was highly decorated, WWI hero Captain George Wallis Hamilton, and the story of his death, along with his gunnery sergeant, George Russell Martin, represented the event's only true fatalities, which marred the event on day one – June 26.

Several of the Marine aviators arriving at the encampment were not having a good day. One of the fighters was involved in a hard-landing in the Wheatfield (there were no injuries) in the process of trying to make a landing near Little Round Top. The aircraft struck a small mound of earth, and there were no reported injuries.[19]

Another fighter suffered a more-damaging hard landing after nearly running out of fuel, forcing the pilot to land in a swampy field on a the farm of Elmer Wagner, about two and a half miles east of York Springs, according to *The Gettysburg Times*.[20]

The fighter was being piloted by Second Lieutenant Benjamin Reisweber, along with his observer, Captain Wade Martin. The newspaper wrote that, upon landing, "The trucks [wheels] under the machine were broken in passing over a ditch and the machine turned over, throwing both men out." The impact also broke the airplane's propeller as well.[21]

**Right:** A "Kite" observation balloon deployed over the U.S.S. Corsair at Brent, France, during World War I.
**Below:** One of the two "kite" or "captive" observation balloons brought by the Marines to Gettysburg can be seen here partially inflated. One of the balloons was slated for destruction during the event, having been condemned by the Navy. The terms kite and captive refer to the balloons being tethered and not free-flying.

The two Marine aviators were taken to the Wagner house and local Doctor E.W. Cashman was summoned to the scene. Martin was determined to have been uninjured in the crash, but Reisweber had sustained a cut on his chin and another cut on his cheek "which required five stitches to close...the camp here was notified and a surgeon from the Hospital Corps brought the two men back to camp in an automobile."[22]

But the worst incident had occurred about the same time as the others or shortly before.

## A tragic beginning

As the arriving columns of troops, along with the vehicles that had accompanies them on the trek from Quantico, marched up Emmitsburg Road and then up West Confederate Avenue to reach the encampment below the Virginia monument on June 26, a disaster was in the making above their heads, which would mar the event for the Marines already on-site, or soon to be.

The column had begun to arrive at the encampment around 8:30 a.m. in a steady stream. As the troops, having all arrived around 12:30 p.m., began to settle down, unload and/or unpack their equipment and pitch camp, there was a resounding crash heard and a plume of smoke spotted around 1 p.m. just north of the encampment in the area of what today is known today as Colt Park.

The cause of it would send shock waves throughout the encampment that would last for several days.

Captain Hamilton, in command of a squadron of fighters providing "scout duty" while escorting the Marine infantry, along with Gunnery Sergeant Martin, were flying a DH-4B fighter at the head of the Marine Fifth Regiment with two other planes, or at the rear of a squadron of four planes (again, discrepancies exist), as they left their encampment at Thurmont shortly after noon on July 26 and proceeded north.[23]

Some discrepancies have to be allowed when considering eyewitness accounts of individuals who had just witnessed a disastrous event unfold before their own eyes.

According to *The Sun,* "His De Haviland (*sic*) was at the rear of a formation of four planes" serving as air scouts" for the Marines marching from Thurmont to Gettysburg. The pilots of the other planes flying Hamilton's squad were identified in the newspaper article as Captain F. P. Mulcahey, Lieutenant William J. Wallace, and Lieutenant W.D. Culberson (*sic*). *The Sun* account stands out as perhaps the more reliable since they were also able to specifically name the pilots in Hamilton's squadron.[24]

Sequence of photographs showing a Martin MBT during a torpedo launch in 1920 near the confluence of the Anacostia and the Potomac rivers, opposite Washington, D.C.

"Everybody saw the plane fluttering earthward like a falling leaf. 'Look at that acrobat,' they cried...Next moment she plunged nose-down behind a clump of trees, the motor roared sharply and then there was an explosion."

*– The (Baltimore) Sun,* June 27, 1922[26]

Underwood & Underwood photograph of the wreckage of the DH-4B in which aviator George Wallis Hamilton and George Russell Martin died June 26, 1922.

The wreckage of the de Havilland in which two aviators lost their lives is loaded aboard a truck as it is being removed from the site of the Lew Defour Carnival. What appears to be the backs of the carnival tents along Steinwehr can be seen in the photograph as well.

Nothing amiss among the planes of the squadron was noticed until the flights began to approach the landing site at Camp Harding. Two of the planes in the escort landed safely in a designated portion of the fields near the intersection of Long Lane and Emmitsburg Road.[25]

*The (Gettysburg) Star and Sentinel* reported, "Eyewitnesses to the accident saw the plane in company with two other aircraft maneuvering over the site of the marine encampment a short time before when suddenly from a height of about 3,000 feet, the plane, carrying Captain Hamilton and Sergeant Martin, was seen going into a nose dive which later developed into a tail spin, bearing the two men to their deaths."[27]

*Aviation* magazine reported, "According to Capt. John Craige, Aide to General LeJeune, who had just stepped out of a Marine Corps plane when he heard a formation of five planes overhead, Captain Hamilton, the leader in a DH4 (*Editor's Note: actually a DH4B*) signaled that he was about to land and cut his engine. From a height of about 500 ft. the plane went into a low spin from which the pilot was seen to partially regain control, apparently about 100 feet from the ground."[28]

Craige, in the article, stated that the plane appeared to have begun to come out of the spin while "descending in a low downward curve," when "'I heard the engine start up with a roar, but feared for the safety of the fliers, they were so near the ground," The Marine witness then added, "When about 100 ft. off the ground Hamilton pulled the stick back to level off, and would have been safe with 50 or 100 ft. more altitude, but just as the plane started to nose upward it struck the ground and was smashed to kindling."[29]

*Leatherneck Magazine* reported, "As the crippled plane descended, at a rate of approximately 200 miles an hour...(it impacted the crash site) striking the ground at an angle of 45 degrees. Several hundred persons witnessed the fatal plunge."[30]

The plane crashed on the William Johns farm around 1:05 p.m., near what is presently the intersection of Johns Avenue and Culp Street in the Colt Park development, and likely in the vicinity of the Johns farm house, which still stands. *The Star and Sentinel* further stated the impact occurred within 50 feet of tents and equestrian equipment belonging to the Lew Dufour Carnival, which had set-up along Steinwehr Avenue.[31]

*The Sun* further reported also that the plane had crashed "nose-down behind a clump of trees...behind Lou Duford's (*sic*) carnival, not more than 20 feet away from the merry-go-round, which, with a lot of sideshows and carnival apparatus, had pitched tents near the marine camp. The carnival grounds were full of people."[32]

*The Star and Sentinel* reported that Martin was pulled from the wreckage, "bleeding profusely from a wound in his head," but alive. Hamilton was found deceased within the wreckage. "Both bodies were hurried into a civilian automobile and rushed to Warner Hospital (Annie M. Warner Hospital, now incorporated into Gettysburg Hospital)." The newspaper also reported, erroneously by all other accounts, that Martin "was dead before the car reached the institution."[33]

*The Sun* reported that Martin had died *after* reaching the hospital, and, further, identified the driver of the "civilian automobile" as Lieutenant Howard Enyart, leader of the Expeditionary Force Marine Band.[34]

According to *The Sun*, Lieutenant Enyart "was driving along the road just outside the carnival grounds when the plane dropped. He and Captain Sullivan, rushed in and found Hamilton and Martin imprisoned in the wreckage. Hamilton was in a brand new uniform to celebrate the end of the marine hike," the *Sun* reported. "Both men had to be cut out from the mass of tangled wires."[35]

The newspaper reported that Enyart had previously known Hamilton, but could not immediately recognize him due to the extent of the pilot's injuries in the wrecked plane. "...he had to look at his identification card" to find out who the deceased pilot was. Enyart then placed Hamilton's body, along with Martin, into his car and quickly drove the short distance from the crash site to Gettysburg (*aka Warner*) Hospital.[36]

*The Sun* further reported, "Martin begged for water on the way. He died just after reaching the hospital, while Chaplain Edward B. Niver was administering the last rites," adding, "Three enlisted men of the aviation section, who knew Hamilton well, stood in the hospital reception room in dungarees weeping like chilrden (sic)."[37]

The wreck was placed on a truck and transported to the encampment site around 4:15 p.m., as was another plane that had gone down earlier during the day near York Springs.[38]

Assessing the damages, the command elected to repair the plane from York Springs, but Hamilton's plane was beyond restoring (the wreck having been described as having been "crushed into a ball about ten feet in diameter)," and a decision was then made

to sell the metal from wreckage of Hamilton's plane, including the metal parts and wiring, according to *The Gettysburg Times*.[39]

The observation that the wreck appeared to be "crushed into a ball about ten feet in diameter" must have been the result of how the wreckage was loaded, or piled-up after unloading, as the airplane does not have that appearance based on photographs of the plane taken at the actual crash site.

The newspaper stated that the metal was sold the following morning (June 27) to a "local junk dealer for 20 cents per 100 pounds...There were several hundred pounds of twisted metal and wire." The sale did not include the engine, which was recovered by the Marine Aviation Corps. To separate the metal from the rest of the airplane, the wrecked fighter was set on fire, a blaze which consumed the torn canvas and wood.[40]

*The Gettysburg Times* also noted that, as the wreckage portions that had been sold left the encampment site, "The twisted mass of wire and bent metal attracted considerable attention when it passed through Lincoln Square. "The drove of the wagon was asked to stop while local souvenir hunters cut pieces of metal from the twisted mass." Immediately after the accident, Brigadier General Butler appointed a board of inquest to investigate the cause of the crash, which included Captain Lewis J. Bourne, Captain James T. Moore, and First Lieutenant H.C. Major. The group convened on the evening of the crash.[41]

*Leatherneck Magazine* also stated in their coverage, "In the opinion of the accompanying aviators, the accident was due to the difference in the reading of the altimeter, by which fliers estimate their distance from the ground, at Quantico and Gettysburg. Quantico is on sea level, while Gettysburg is 600 feet above sea level. Consequently, when the altimeter reads 1,000 feet at the latter place, the actual distance is only 400 feet."[42]

Hamilton and Martin were regarded as having been killed in the line-of-duty in the service of their country, and the deaths of the two Marines may have been the only (to present time) military line-of-duty deaths that have occurred on the Gettysburg

> "...the death of another hero warrior who had added his death to the thousands who three score years ago poured their life blood on that very ground. Beside him lay another fighting man from whom life was ebbing fast, as it had done so often in the long ago. Again forms of dead and dying were carried from the field."

battlefield since 1863.[43]

Marine officers stated that they believed Hamilton tried his best to avoid the crowds at the carnival, knowing his plane was in trouble, and that the aircraft could have struck the carnival itself if he had continued to try and maneuver the plane out of its plunge toward the earth, "and possibly kill many people in the resulting crash," *The Gettysburg Times* wrote.[45]

## The Last to Fall…

Capt. George W. Hamilton and his gunnery sergeant, George Russell Martin, were the only Marine fatalities suffered during the course of the summer maneuvers held on the battlefields of Gettysburg in 1922.

Much of the attention and media coverage of the tragic and fatal crash of the de Havilland DH-4B that Hamilton piloted that fateful day on June 26 focused on the captain, a decorated WWI hero (he had served in the Marine infantry in the war), while Martin's death was, sadly, less covered and less lamented by the media in general. Martin had not served in WWI.

Nevertheless, they both ultimately sacrificed their lives in the line-of-duty, no doubt both looking forward to activities and maneuvers planned for the event when their plane fell from the sky, the resulting crash casting a "darkness" over the entire encampment, as an estimated thousand Marines rushed to the scene, from all points of the camp, to see what could be done, if anything, for the two pilots who lie entangled in the wreckage.

## Captain George W. Hamilton

Capt. George W. Hamilton, age 29, was born in Washington, D.C., in July 5, 1892, to British-born Charles A. and Ida Margaret Hamilton, and had one brother, Charles Burwell, and two sisters, Mary Elizabeth and Margaret Dorothy. His mother passed away in 1918, following an unsuccessful surgery to treat an unspecified ailment. He would gave turned 30 on the day the Marines were schedule to being leaving the Gettysburg battlefield following the maneuvers.[46]

Hamilton commanded the Forty-Ninth Compa-

"Last Night of the War," painted by Frederick C. Yohn, depicts the Fifth Marine Regiment crossing the Meuse River in 1918. Captain George Wallis Hamilton is depicted in the center with his hand on his helmet. France awarded him two medals of honor (Croix de Guerre), and a host of American medals, for his heroism helping to end the German advance on Paris.

**Left:** Captain George Wallis Hamilton. **Below:** Capt. Hamilton's death certificate.

Form V. S. No. 9—25M—10-21-30.

COMMONWEALTH OF PENNSYLVANIA
DEPARTMENT OF HEALTH
BUREAU OF VITAL STATISTICS

**CERTIFICATE OF DEATH**

File No. 59471

1. PLACE OF DEATH

County of _Adams_
Township of _Cumberland_
Borough of
City of                    (No.                    St.,                    Ward)

Registration District No. _106_
Primary Registration District No. _2010_
Registered No. _74_

(If death occurred in a Hospital or Institution, give its NAME instead of street and number.)

2. FULL NAME _George W. Hamilton_

| PERSONAL AND STATISTICAL PARTICULARS | MEDICAL CERTIFICATE OF DEATH |
|---|---|

3. SEX _M_
4. COLOR OR RACE _White_
5. SINGLE, MARRIED, WIDOWED OR DIVORCED (Write the word) _Single_

16. DATE OF DEATH _June 26, 1922_

6. DATE OF BIRTH _July 5 1892_ (Month) (Day) (Year)

17. I HEREBY CERTIFY, That I attended deceased from _____ 192_, to _____ 192_.
that I last saw _____ alive on _June 26, 1922_,
and that death occurred, on the date stated above, at _1:10 P._ M.
The CAUSE OF DEATH* was as follows:
_multiple injuries incident to airplane crash (comp fracture vault & base of cranium_ ___)

7. AGE _29_ yrs. _11_ mos. _22_ ds.
If LESS than 1 day ... hrs. or ... min.?

8. OCCUPATION
(a) Trade, profession, or particular kind of work _Capt. U.S.M.C._
(b) General nature of industry, business, or establishment in which employed (or employer)

Contributory (Secondary)

(Duration) _188_ yrs. ___ mos. ___ ds.

9. BIRTHPLACE (State or Country) _Washington D.C._

(Signed) _Herbert L. Shine_
6/26 1922 (Address) _Lieut. M.C. U.S.N. Quantico, Va_

PARENTS
10. NAME OF FATHER _Chas. A. Hamilton_
11. BIRTHPLACE OF FATHER (State or Country) _unknown_
12. MAIDEN NAME OF MOTHER _unknown_
13. BIRTHPLACE OF MOTHER (State or Country) _unknown_

*State the DISEASE CAUSING DEATH, or in deaths from VIOLENT CAUSES, state (1) MEANS OF INJURY; and (2) whether ACCIDENTAL, SUICIDAL, or HOMICIDAL.

18. LENGTH OF RESIDENCE (For Hospitals, Institutions, Transients or Recent Residents).
At place of death ... yrs. ... mos. ... ds.    In the State ... yrs. ... mos. ... ds.
Where was disease contracted, if not at place of death?
Former or usual residence _Washington D.C._

14. THE ABOVE IS TRUE TO THE BEST OF MY KNOWLEDGE.
(Informant) _Herbert L. Shine, M.D._
(Address) _Quantico, Va_

15.
Filed _6/26_ 1922 _Henry Strauss_ Local Registrar

19. PLACE OF BURIAL, OR REMOVAL _Washington D.C._   DATE OF BURIAL _June 27 1922_
20. UNDERTAKER _H.B. Bender_   ADDRESS _Gettysburg Pa_

**Right:** Gunnery Sergeant George Russell Martin. **Below:** GySgt. Martin's death certificate.

Form V. S. No. 5—5000—10-21-20.

COMMONWEALTH OF PENNSYLVANIA
DEPARTMENT OF HEALTH
BUREAU OF VITAL STATISTICS

CERTIFICATE OF DEATH

1. PLACE OF DEATH
County of *Adams*
Township of *Gettysburg*
or
Borough of
or
City of

Registration District No. *106*
Primary Registration District No. *1006*
Registered No. *75*

File No. *59468*

(If death occurred in a Hospital or Institution, give its NAME instead of street and number.)

2. FULL NAME *Martin, George Russell*

PERSONAL AND STATISTICAL PARTICULARS

MEDICAL CERTIFICATE OF DEATH

3. SEX *Male*  4. COLOR OR RACE *White U.S.*  5. SINGLE, MARRIED, WIDOWED OR DIVORCED (Write the word) *Single*

16. DATE OF DEATH *June 26, 1922*

6. DATE OF BIRTH *September 15, 1899*

7. AGE yrs. *22*  mos. *9*  ds. *11*  If LESS than 1 day how many .....hrs. or .....min.?

17. I HEREBY CERTIFY, That I attended deceased from .....192.. to .....192..
that I last saw ..... alive on *June 26,* 192*2*
and that death occurred, on the date stated above, at *11.30 P.* M.
The CAUSE OF DEATH was as follows:
*Multiple injuries incident to airplane crash (fracture base of skull — penetrating wound spinal dural cavity*
Contributory
*via perineum*

8. OCCUPATION
(a) Trade, profession, or particular kind of work *Gy. Sgt. USMC*
(b) General nature of industry, business, or establishment in which employed (or employer)

9. BIRTHPLACE (State or Country) *Buffalo, N.Y.*

10. NAME OF FATHER *Joseph J. Martin*

11. BIRTHPLACE OF FATHER (State or Country) *unknown*

12. MAIDEN NAME OF MOTHER *unknown*

13. BIRTHPLACE OF MOTHER (State or Country) *unknown*

(Duration) *188* yrs. ..... mos. ..... ds.
(Signed) *Herbert L. Shine*
*Lieut. M.C. USN*
*6/28 1922* (Address) *Quantico, Va.*

*State the Disease Causing Death; or in deaths from Violent Causes, state (1) Means or Injury; and (2) whether Accidental, Suicidal, or Homicidal.

18. LENGTH OF RESIDENCE (For Hospitals, Institutions, Transients or Recent Residents).
At place of death ..... yrs. ..... mos. ..... ds. In the State ..... yrs. ..... mos. ..... ds.
Where was disease contracted, if not at place of death?
Former or usual residence *Buffalo N.Y.*

14. THE ABOVE IS TRUE TO THE BEST OF MY KNOWLEDGE.
(Informant) *Herbert L. Shine, MD*
(Address) *Quantico, Va.*

15.

Filed *June 28, 1922* *Henry Skeuch* Local Registrar

19. PLACE OF BURIAL OR REMOVAL *Buffalo N.Y.*  DATE OF BURIAL *June 28, 1922*

20. UNDERTAKER *A.B. Snider Gettysburg Pa*

ny of the Fifth Marines during WWI. He was promoted to captain in 1917, and "served in the Verdon Sector and Chateau Thierry and Soissons, in 1918," according to *Aviation* magazine. "As second in command of the First Battalion of the Famous Fifth from July 8 he saw active service in the Marbache Sector (Point-a-Mousson) from Aug. 7 to 16, having become a temporary Major on July 1."[47]

The magazine further reported, "From Sept. 12 to 16 he was in the St. Mihiel offensive and in the Meuse-Argonne drive from Nov. 1 to 11, going to the Rhine later in the year, where he remained until May 1919."[48]

Troops under Hamilton's command reportedly fired the last shots of WWI, "not receiving news of armistice until 1 p.m., Nov. 11, 1918," according to *Who's Who in the Nation's Capital 1921-1922*.[49]

Hamilton resigned from the Marine Corps in 1919, after having served in Washington, at Marine headquarters, and in Haiti and Santa Domingo in the Dominican Republic. He reenlisted into the marine

> **"It was the first full military funeral accorded a deceased member of the United States forces here since 1918 and attracted scores of people, along the streets from the church to the Reading railroad station."**
> *- The Gettysburg Times* **June 28, 1922**[53]

aviation section in 1922, three months before his death in Gettysburg."[50]

As a result of his heroic actions during WWI, Hamilton received a number of honors from two countries. France awarded him the Croix de Guerre twice, the first time for his involvement in the capture of Blanc Mount in the Meuse-Argonne offensive, and a second for his participation in the crossing of the Meuse before the armistice.[51]

From the United States government, Hamilton received the Navy Cross and two Distinguished Service Crosses for his gallantry at Chateau Thierry on June 6, 1918, at which time he rallied the Forty-Ninth Company, and prompted a charge, which he personally spear-headed, against some 20 German troops who had been spotted moving machine guns forward to assault his position, resulting in their capture. By the time the Germans organized a series of counter-attacks, the Forty-Ninth had been reinforced and the Germans gave up.[52]

The captain also received a number of other

Photograph of the area in which the June 26, 1922, fatal airplane crash occurred. This was a vacant lot at the time, occupied only by the Lew Dufour Carnival, which had set-up fronting on Steinwehr Avenue.

medals, including four distinguished Service Crosses, and citations for his efforts during the "war to end all wars." His acclaim led him to be listed in the *Who's Who in the Nation's Capital* for 1921-1922. His father was also listed, being a congressional news reporter.[54]

Hamilton was interred in the Arlington National Cemetery on June 29 with "full military honors," following a funeral service held at Central High School, from which he had graduated in 1912. *Aviation* magazine noted, "…at the request of his sister, so planes flew over the National Cemetery in connection with the services."[55]

## Gunnery Sergeant George Russell Martin

GySgt. George Russell Martin was born on September 15, 1899, in Buffalo, N. Y., the son of Joseph J. and Anna Martin. The father's name was erroneously identified as Charles in the June 28 edition of *The Gettysburg Times*.[56]

Martin enlisted in the Marine Corps at age 20, on October 11, 1919, wherein he served in aviation at Quantico and in Santa Domingo in the Dominican Republic.

He was a graduate of the U.S. Navy Aviation Quartermaster School in Great Lakes, Illinois, and was honorably discharged as a sergeant on October 10, 1921, after serving out his term of enlistment, and had been awarded the Good Conduct Medal. Martin then re-enlisted in the Marine Corps on February 15, 1922, again in the Marine aviation service.

Following his death at the Gettysburg Hospital (aka Warner) on June 26, his remains were turned over to Harry B. Bender, a Gettysburg undertaker.

*The Gettysburg Times* described the conveyance of Martin's body to Saint Francis Xavier Roman Catholic Church on June 28 as thus:

"To the strains of 'Nearer My God to Thee,' played by the post band, the casket enshrouded in American flag, containing the body of Sergeant Martin was removed from the undertaking parlor of H.B. Bender and Son, Baltimore street, to St. Francis Xavier church, West High street. As the body was being taken from the funeral parlor to the waiting hearse outside, and the band played the secular selection, two squads of eight men each, stood at present arms.

When the casket had been placed in the hearse, the cortege moved slowly to Xavier church while the band played a dirge. The six pallbearers flanked the hearse.

At the church as the casket was being taken from the hearse, the band again played 'Nearer My God to Thee' while the other members of the funeral party stood at attention. The same ceremony took place when the body was brought out of the church."[57]

The service at the church was conducted by Catholic chaplain Captain Joseph F. Underwood, attached to the Marines' Fourth Brigade, presiding, with the Revered Father Mark Stock assisting.[58]

The funeral procession subsequently proceeded from the church to the railroad station, accompanied by the Expeditionary Force Marine Band. "Businesses halted along the line of march while the funeral procession passed," the *Times* recorded. "Throngs stood with bared heads as the funeral cortege passed."

The body of the aviator was then "placed aboard the 10 o'clock train for Harrisburg over the Philadelphia and Reading railroad" to be taken back to Buffalo, accompanied by "six comrades from his company at Camp Harding, who had served as the pallbearers…under the command of First Sergeant McDonnell," the newspaper reported.[59]

Martin's body was then shipped back to Buffalo, where he was buried in the Forest Lawn Cemetery on June 28, following a second military service, this time in his hometown.

Marine Cadet George W. Hamilton (top) and GySgt. George Russell Martin (bottom) in pictures that ran in newspapers after their deaths.

"The glittering rays of a summer day's sun play hide and seek with marble slabs and bronze statues dotting the countryside. The marines are here, there and everywhere. In tactical maneuvers they charge, and in great khaki lines tread the ground hallowed long ago."

*– The Washington Post,*

*June 30, 1922.* [1]

# CHAPTER 5

# MANUEVERS BEGIN

The column of Marines had successfully trekked more than 80 miles, marching from Quanitico, Virginia, to Washington, D.C., into suburban and rural Maryland, and finally across the Mason-Dixon Line into Pennsylvania, arriving in Cumberland Township, the location of their immense encampment and site of the July 3, 1863, battle that came to be known as Pickett's Charge, adjacent to Gettysburg Borough, on June 26.

Seemingly immeasurable tonnage of equipment was hauled by the Marines on their march, or was shipped to the site by trucks, airplanes, and by rail in order to support the encampment and the military maneuvers from June 26 through July 5, during which mock combat would occur almost every day, along with more than 5,000 mouths to feed three times daily.

In the end, this would be more than just another Marine exercise and military demonstration to promote the Corps. The Marines were, for all intent and purposes, making history, one separate from, but at the same time, a part of that infamous battlefield dating back to a time already 59 years *"Gone with the Wind..."*

Pages 96-97: Marines pose for a group photograph at Devil's Den during one of the "mandatory"t ours conducted to teach the troops about the Battle of Gettysburg, a portion of which they would soon be reenacting. Page 98 Top: General John Joseph "Black Jack" Pershing, President Warren Harding, Lieutenant General John Archer Lejeune , General Smedley Darlington Butler at Camp Harding, July 1, 1922. Page 98 Bottom: Marine artillery at Gettysburg, 1922. Above: John Archer Lejeune.

## A "pall" over the camp

Dirty, hungry, and just plain tuckered out, more than 5,000 foot-sore Marines marched to their final objective of the long 80-mile hike from Quantico – the "hallowed grounds" that had served as the site of the American Civil War's most deadly three-day engagement – the Gettysburg Battlefield.

The first sign that the column of Marines was approaching the encampment on the battlefield was the arrival around 8:30 a.m., June 26, of the mounted Pennsylvania State Police, who had escorted the head of the column from the Mason-Dixon Line to the battlefield, and a motorcade of Marine officers, including Brigadier General Smedley D. Butler, followed by the Marine Motor Transport Corps, the signal corps, and the military police.[2]

They had traveled to the battlefield from Emmitsburg Road, where they then swung onto West Confederate Avenue and into the encampment which was laid out along the avenue's eastern side.[3]

On the heels of the initial arrivals was the column of thousands of Marines of the Fifth and Sixth Regiments, along with the equipment that had made the trip with them, who proceeded to arrive "in almost a continuous procession" for four hours, the last of whom arrived and entered the encampment around 12:30 p.m. The Marine column, *The Gettysburg Times* noted, was so long that it took more than half an hour for the column to pass any one point along the line-of-march.[4]

The celebratory arrival of the Marine column

Marine signalmen in France, 1917, along with two French soldiers who are wearing berets.

was suddenly marred by the deaths of Marine aviator Captain George Wallis Hamilton, along with Gunnery Sergeant George Russell Martin, which had occurred in a fatal airplane crash just north of the Marine compound.

"It was the end of the long trail up from Quantico," *The (Baltimore) Sun* reported, "and the leathernecks were singing and cheering past the silent ranks of monuments that mark the victories and defeats of Gettysburg...But for the rest of the day there was no happiness among the marines... (who were) were plunged in gloom and talked of nothing but the deaths of Captain Hamilton and Gunnery Sergeant Martin."[5]

According to *The Gettysburg Times*, "Everything was quiet in the camp of the Air Corps, where the death of two of their men, in the plane crash Monday afternoon (June 26), as well as the injury to Lieutenant Benjamin Reisweber, in another accident, is probably more keenly felt than in any other section of the large camp."[6]

But in spite of the dismal pall that hung like a dark cloud over the encampment, there remained

> "The march was like that of a conquering army returning from the battlefields, as thousands of motorists were gathered at every crossroads to cheer the troops on their way."
>
> *- The Gettysburg Times* June 26, 1922.[7]

much work yet to be done to prepare the site for the coming events, and the Marines did their best to help finish whatever tasks needed to be completed in order to make the camp inhabitable for the Marines and a host of guests, and to prepare the fields for the upcoming maneuvers and military demonstrations.

The officers apparently did not push the troops too hard, the day having marked the conclusion of a long march, followed by a tragic beginning to their ten-day stay on the old "bloody fields of glory" that had, itself, witnessed a national tragedy 59 years prior.

*The Gettysburg Times* reported the arrival of an additional 500 Marines, attached to the Atlantic Fleet, who had been brought into the maneuvers, in addition to those who marched in the main column. Their purpose was to "fill out the ranks of the Fifth and Sixth Regiments, taking the places of the men whose terms of enlistment have expired."[8]

Chaplain Niven, who had administered last rights to GySgt. Martin as Martin lay dying in the Warner (Gettysburg) Hospital, declined to put up the movie screen that evening and canceled the movie that had been planned for the Marines in respect for the memories of the deceased.[9]

The exhausted Marines at least had a restful night under the Gettysburg skies. "The men in Camp Harding...are sleeping under 'pup' tents, which they described as being comfortable, on the first night here...The grass in the field occupied by the camp had just been recently mown and left to lay, serving as a soft bed on which the blankets were spread. The Sea Soldiers are well pleased with the location of their camp...," *The Gettysburg Times* wrote.[10]

**An educational process**

The commanders in charge of the "expedition" felt that it would be necessary, in order to properly portray Pickett's Charge during July 1, 3, and 4, that the soldiers should know the particulars concerning the events that had occurred on the grounds 59 years ago.

"Different guides may tell different marines different things, but this historical pageant will not end before this whole marine brigade is agreed that Pickett picked a tough place for his charge (*Editor's Note: Confederate General Robert E. Lee ultimately selected the field for the attack, not General Pickett.*)," *The Sun* wrote. "Brig.-Gen. Smedley D. Butler is determined that his men shall know the real history of the battle of Gettysburg before they fight it again. They will be handicapped...by an official guide battalion that has found the battle of Gettysburg commonplace and has trimmed it up to suit modern tourists."[11]

On June 28, *The Sun* reported that two battalions of Marines toured the battlefield aboard 20 trucks, with an "official guide" in each. The Marine command would have these tours conducted, up to July 1, in a manner so as to not overwhelm the guides."[12] *The Sun* described the initial aftermath of just such a tour, and the lectures given by the guides, in the wake of a tour given on June 28:

"As a result of the tour there was much unrest in camp tonight. Some marines were calling Hooker a fool for telling Pickett to charge. Other marines declared Hooker didn't tell Pickett any such thing, that Hooker was in one army and Pickett in another.

Marines attended a number of on-site lectures on the history of the Gettysburg battlefield as part of their indoctrination into the methods of the military of the period.

Marines pose at the High Water Mark for a photograph during the 1922 maneuvers.

"Then there are groups of soldiers of the sea who have themselves turned sightseers. Go anywhere through the twenty-five-mile area of Gettysburg battleground now and you see them gazing reverently at likenesses of men who wrote pages of history to which the very men now encamped here have added many a brilliant chapter."

*– The Washington Post, 30 June, 1922.*[13]

# THE TOUR STARTS HERE...

*The (Baltimore) Sun* reporter Raymond S. Tompkins wrote about battlefield tour guides, jokingly, after climbing aboard one of the Marine vehicles and joining the soldiers for a tour of the battlefield, stating, "There are about 100 of these guides in Gettysburg. Some estimates put it as high as 250."

"Nobody seems to know accurately, because official licensed, ordained and confirmed guides (you have to get everything from a personal letter from the President to the laying-on-of-hands by an archbishop before you can be one, according to the guides themselves) pop-up out of every cellar and lurk around every corner," he wrote.

"They all insist they tell the truth, the whole truth and nothing but the truth, and they insist it before you ask them, evidently feeling that you suspect them…they can't help showing people around the place…like side-show men exploiting the fattest woman in the world, positively, or the wildest man that ever lived in Borneo, absolutely," Tompkins stated.

The tour guide leading that which the reporter had attended went on to list all the mistakes that almost all the generals had made during the battle, Tompkins commenting, "…the Marines went back to camp just about certain that the Battle of Gettysburg ought to have been called the 'Battle of Mistakes'…(and that the battle of 1863) should have been fought by the official, ordained and accepted guides…"

*The Sun* reporter concluded that, regardless of the "official" indoctrination of the Marines regarding the battle, the exposure had nevertheless peeked their interest. "Every evening you can see them in pairs or little groups, trailing off into the woods to look for some new monument with some new story of those days upon it. They go without guides. They go alone, like priests in to their alters."[14]

# Provisions and supplies

The task of providing provisions and supplies for the long encampment commenced even before the column of more than 5,000 Marines that had left their base at Quantico.

Napoleon once said (although the quote is also attributed to Frederick the Great), "An Army marches on its stomach," but if that is true, it should also be added that an army also camps on its stomach.

A fair amount of the provisions the men would need on their trek through three states and the District of Columbia had been supplied through previously existing long-term contracts, and were transported with the column in various vehicles, both motorized and hand-drawn.[15]

However, those supplies along would not support more than 5,000 troops in the long encampment that lie ahead of them, and the Corps then relied upon local farmers and merchants for additional supplies.

By June 19, the Marines had already granted contracts to local farmers and merchants for supplies of the voluminous amount of wood and ice that would be needed from June 26 through July 6, and advertisements had begun to appear in the local newspapers soliciting bids for even more provisions.[16]

One such group of solicitations appeared in print in which the Marines were seeking 16,000 pounds of hay and 13,300 pounds of oats, leading *The Gettysburg Times* to speculate that "some horses are included in the outfit," although the Marines were largely mechanized and not as reliant on horse-power as they had been throughout World War I. A number of horses were used,

however, during the July reenactments by field officers and the hospital corps.[17]

*The (Baltimore) Sun* further noted that Marine Major Jeter R. Horton, and his quartermaster clerk, Harry Halladay, based their preliminary provision and supplies estimates premised on "that 6,000 persons must be fed for one week."[18]

"Halladay today (June 27) ordered 100 more cases of fresh eggs and 3,000 pounds of bacon. He will order 4,500 more pounds of bacon in a day or so," *The Sun* reported. "He has received a carload of fresh beef, and has ordered 3,000 pounds of frankfurters, 3,000 pounds of pork sausage, a carload of potatoes, one-half a carload of milk (to which fresh milk will be added every day) and he has 100,000 pounds of such staples as beans, coffee, rice, tea and sugar on hand."[19]

Additionally, the newspaper noted, Halladay acquired bread for the encampment from whichever major cities lie nearest to the Gettysburg battlefield, "at the rate of nearly 7,000 pounds a day. He gets ice cream and vegetables the same way," the newspaper stated.[20]

"Things were a little different in 1863," *The Sun* commented. "The Confederate Army had to steal cattle to eat and shoes to wear on its way to the original Battle of Gettysburg, and it got no ice cream."[21]

**Below left:** Marines peeling potatoes (or beets, which were boiled and used to simulate blood during the battles) in Camp Harding. **Below right:** Marines relax and enjoy a meal outside their pup tents in Camp Harding.

Then another argument started up on the side for the theory that they were both in the same army, but that Pickett had got on the wrong side and had to charge to get back where he belonged.

"Before taps, they had killed General Armistead in 40 different ways, and had the 'devils den,' the peach orchard and the 'bloody angle' all mixed up with Antietam, Chancellorsville, and Valley Forge.

"But they will be straightened out before they are through. Two battalions are to go on this tour each day, and the same guides will accompany them, and all the marines will have to do will be to remember what the guides tell 'em and stick to it."[22]

While making an effort to get the Marines to understand the battle and to *think* like Civil War soldiers, the next challenge was to get them to *look* like Civil War soldiers, and ultimately to *fight* like Civil War soldiers.

Since most would be portraying Confederate forces in the upcoming reenactments of Pickett's Charge, the color of their uniforms, being a brown, could readily pass as butternut, the color of the uniforms worn by some Confederate units that had been achieved by dying cloth with oil from the bark of the butternut tree.[23]

With that, half the clothing battle was essentially won by default. However, half was not enough for the U.S. Marine Corps.

"The entire infantry brigade came forth in the rain this afternoon (June 28), and lined up along Seminary Ridge. As far as they were able they had taken the latest Marine uniform and turned it into a Confederate costume," *The Sun* wrote. "They had left off their leggings and pulled their gray socks up over their trousers, and kept 'em up with safety pins. They had altered the shape of their campaign hats, creasing them in the center instead of pinching 'em into peaks. They looked as much like the Confederate Army as it is possible for young men to look who have to shave every day."[24]

The Marines were already accustomed to carrying blanket rolls on campaign marches, so they merely dawned these rolls for Confederate reenactment purposes as well.

Admiring the outcome of the effort to convert the Marines into Confederate soldiers, *The Washington Post* reported, "The first 'dress rehearsal' for Pickett's charge was held this afternoon (June 28). It was a transformed brigade of marine infantry that formed on the heights of Seminary Ridge."[25]

Field officers also spent time studying the

"Cyclorama of the Battle of Gettysburg" to get an overview of how the grand spectacle of Pickett's Charge may have looked. The immense, panoramic painting was executed by artist Paul Dominique Philippoteaux and his assistants, the finished product first exhibited in Chicago in 1883.[26]

**The call "to arms"**

*The Washington Post* reported, "Camp Harding is slowly recovering from the shock of yesterday's two casualties." On the morning of June 27, with the first of the Pickett's Charge reenactment just four days away, the Marines had to set-aside the feelings of melancholy that generally follow on the heels of a dismal experience, focus on the business of waging war.[27]

As part of the training exercises, officers planned spontaneous engagements to which various Marine units would be ordered to immediately react, and were to occur at any time. The idea behind the scramble-into-action concept was to provide command, control, and deployment challenges while in hostile territory.

"These orders, assimilating the conditions of actual warfare, are sent out from Camp Headquarters, properly known as Marine Corps Expeditionary Force Headquarters, without previous advice and for immediate execution," *The (Gettysburg) Star and Sentinel* reported.[28]

But before any widespread maneuvers involving the element of surprise were to begin, the command decided July 27 to send the Marines out in a drill, to familiarize as many as possible with the manner in which troops that took part in the actual Civil War battles. *The Gettysburg Times* stated that two battalions of the Fifth Regiment, which had included nine companies of infantry and three machine gun squads, marched out of camp and toward Oak Ridge to begin their training exercises.[29] Describing this first action, *The Gettysburg Times* wrote:

"Shortly after 1 o'clock, Monday afternoon, the long line of troopers wended their way out of the camp, headed by staff officers and a Company of Signal Corps men. Many of the staff officers were mounted on horses. The Machine Gun Companies presented an interesting appearance to the uninitiated, for instead of carrying rifles, as their comrades in the Infantry, they drew (pulled) small trucks (wagons), each equipped with two pneumatic tired wheels, on which were mounted the guns, while on others of the same style were the ammunition for the guns. These carriages are drawn by two men

**Top:** Marine column crosses the road leading from Vamp Harding to the High Water Mark. The gap in the fence they are passing through is still there. **Bottom:** Marine signalmen on the battlefield during one of the Marine Corps' Civil War reenactments and maneuvers. **Page 107:** Marines charge either participating in a public presentation of Pickett's Charge, or in the act of rehearsing it. The troops rehearsed the battle from June 27 through June 30.

and although they carry a considerable load, are easy to handle.

"The troops marched out West Confederate Avenue, passed the Chambersburg Road to the rolling piece of country in the vicinity of the First Day's battle...The columns were halted some distance beyond the Railroad Cut, where the men were gathered into several hollow squares, in the field, and the officer-instructors addressed them concerning the tactics to be taken up on the afternoon...Following the detailed instructions, the men were given drills by companies and finally by Battalions until the untutored men in the ranks could not be distinguished from the veterans..."[30]

The rain had fallen intermittingly during the day, and would continue to do so, not only the next day, but that only marked the beginning of a series of deluges which would soon turn Camp Harding into a proverbial bog.

On the morning of June 28, the Marine command apparently decided to try one of their "impromptu" call-to-arms, alerting selected groups of Marines that an attack might be eminent.

Units were alerted around dawn when, according to *The Washington Post*, "...aerial scouts reported the presence of a 'hostile' force in the vicini-ty. Marines were soon marching northward along Confederate Avenue to rout the 'enemy.'" The contest was settled relatively quickly and the troops who had been allocated to participate in this faux attack returned to camp.[31]

Subsequently, troops that had been present at the Oak Ridge drill were among those selected for the first rehearsal of Pickett's Charge on the actual 1863 site of the charge, while other units that had not drilled at Oak Ridge were sent there for their initial exercises. All the while, the other groups were being sent on the battlefield tours to learn the historic background concerning the event they would soon be replicating.

Rotating the troops in this manner also helped the unit commanders keep the education and training process manageable, given the numbers of men they had to deal with.

The Oak Ridge drills of July 28 were merely a repeat of those provided at that location the day before, but this day also marked the beginning of the rehearsals for Pickett's Charge. Those assigned to the Pickett's Charge drill also were the first to report "for duty" in their makeshift Confederate attire.[32]

The Marines-turned-reenactors were split into two groups, one representing the attackers, and the other representing the defenders.

"Two battalions from the Fifth and Sixth Regi-

ment (*sic*) were dispatched to the vicinity of High Water Mark, where a 'fence problem' was scheduled for study," *The Gettysburg Times* reported. "The problem consisted of one battalion intrenched (*sic*) on the defense, while the other was detailed to attack the position and take it, in the most approved fashion. Several officers were appointed to act as umpires of the affair and make criticism of the methods used in the attack and whether or not it was done correctly." The "charge" commenced when one of the 75mm artillery guns fired a blank round as the signal to start.[33]

As the attacking troops advanced and clashed with the defenders, other troops began to select key areas of the fields in which to place various military assets that had been brought to the site, including "ground sounders," also known as "big ears," which were listening devices employed to detect the sounds of approaching airplanes.[34]

The "big ear" consisted of two large cones, with the wide, open ends projecting toward the sky, and a headset attacked to the pair at the bottom of each

of the cones. An operator would place the headset on his (or her) head, and could thus discern the sounds of the engines of the aircraft and, with experience, the direction and distance the airplane or group of airplanes was located.

Although seemingly primitive, the arrangement was apparently quite effective, and the "big ears" were even used up into WWII, notably in England, where they allowed soldiers to listen for the approach of German bombers and fighters crossing the English Channel.

In addition to the sounding devices, "antiaircraft (*sic*) guns were being strapped in brotherly fashion to ancient smooth-bore field guns that mark spots where Confederate artillery stood" *The Sun* reported. "More of these old guns had field telephones hanging to their muzzles by late afternoon." *The Gettysburg Times* noted that the aviation group was also busy mounting searchlights, and locating the best positions for truck-mounted anti-aircraft guns.[35]

As Marines, other than those involved in drills

Marine assists one of his "wounded" comrades during Pickett's Charge, 1922.

**Above:** "Big Ears" listening devices were used to detect aircraft in the days before radar. This one is being demonstrated on Bolling Field near the confluence of the Anacostia and the Potomac rivers, opposite Washington, D.C . **Below:** Artillery and "big ears" parked behind Seminary Ridge during the 1922 Gettysburg maneuvers.

# DELEGATES BY THE SCORE

The events that unfolded in July 1922, upon the gently sloping fields and the natural ramparts of diabase hills and ridges around Gettysburg garnered the attention of dignitaries far and wide, who began to arrive just before and during the Marine reenactments of Pickett's Charge.

They came from Washington, D.C., the commonwealths of Pennsylvania and Virginia, the states of Arkansas and Oklahoma, and other countries that included Japan, Venezuela, Brazil, Cuba, the Netherlands, Poland, Great Britain, and Italy. Some came to see the reenactments of the famed historic events of 1863 that unfolded here. Some came to observe the techniques of modern warfare. Some came to see it all.

From the United States, the roll call of military leadership who attended, included many of those who had made history themselves: Acting Secretary of the Navy Theodore Roosevelt, Jr.; General Charles Sawyer; General John J. Pershing; Brigadier General Smedley D. Butler; Major General John A. Lejeune; General Charles D. Dawes; and Marine Major General Wendell C. Neville. From the civil side of governance were Pennsylvania Governor William C. Sproul, U.S. Senator George W. Pepper (Pa.), U.S. Senator John W. Harrell (Okla.), U.S. Senator Thaddeus H. Caraway (Ark.), Speaker of the U.S. House of Representatives Frederick Gillett, and Virginia Governor Lee Trinkle.[36]

From foreign lands came Captain Osami Nagano, attaché from the Japanese Navy, Commander M. Hibine, assistant attaché from the Japanese Navy, Major General H. Haraguchi, Japanese military attaché, Captain Y. Fujii, assistant Japanese military attaché, Captain K. Matsumoto, assistant Japanese military attaché, Lieutenant Diogenes Morcles (*Editor's Note: Also found spelled Morales*), naval attaché from the Venezuelan government, Captain H. Graca Aranha, naval attaché from the Brazilian government, Captain E. A. Varona, Cuban military attaché, Dr. J. B. Hubrecht, Secretary to the Netherlands Legation, Major Cassimer Mach, Polish military attaché, Colonel G.A.L. Dumont, French military attaché, Captain S.R. Bailey, naval attaché from Great Britain, M.G. Christie, British air attaché, Colonel Marquis V. diBernezzo, Italian military attaché, and Captain Carlo Huntington, assistant Italian military attaché.[37]

110

The lists are likely far from complete, and some of the out-of-state congressmen, judges, and others have been omitted herein for brevity purposes.

At least one of the foreign dignitaries would later make history himself, of a more infamous nature. Captain Osami Nagano would become (Japanese) Combined Fleet Commander-in-chief Osami Nagano in 1937. Nineteen years after standing on the fields of Gettysburg observing the Marine assaults, Nagano met with Emperor Hirohito on November 3, 1941, and that meeting resulted in Hirohito authorizing Nagano on November 5, to give the go-ahead to an act that would become known as "a day that will live in infamy" – the attack on Pearl Harbor, December 7, 1941.[38]

Nagano died January 5, 1947, in prison while awaiting his war crimes trial to conclude regarding his responsibility involving the attack on Pearl Harbor.[39]

*Page 110:* President, governors and officers stand in front of the Canvas White House on July 1, 1922. Front row from right to left (not all are identified): Virginia Governor Elbert Lee Trinkle, President Warren Harding, General John Joseph "Black Jack" Pershing, Pennsylvania Governor William C. Sproul, and Lieutenant General John Archer Lejeune. *Below:* Foreign military and attachés' at Camp Harding.

and reenacting, tested their equipment, residents were likely beginning to get a feel for the shape of things to come. Throughout the day, artillery crews fired their 75mm guns, while others tested various types of machine guns. On top of this, literally, the combat aircraft took to the air to practice their "dogfights" and other aerial routines.[40]

The inconvenient rain that had hampered the Marines off-and-on for two days now began to intensify, and the result was that a full-blown, nighttime aerial engagement had to be called off.[41]

## Twentieth-century style

Rehearsals for the upcoming public presentation of Pickett's Charge also continued in earnest on June 29, along with other military exercises, and educational programs intended to inform the Marines of the historic context of the event.

"During the afternoon, another rehearsal of Pickett's charge was conducted, when thirty-six companies of between seventy and one hundred men each, took part in the charge over the mile or more of ground between West Confederate avenue and the stone fence, which marks the Union lines." This rehearsal of the charge constituted one of the largest rehearsals yet, with 36 companies of Ma-

rines, each company comprised of from 70 to 100 men, or between 2,500 and 3,600 troops.[42]

At least one additional, smaller rehearsal of the charge was also held around 3 p.m., after the massive afternoon rehearsal had been concluded. But the twist was, the 3 p.m. rehearsal focused on the "modern" version of the charge to be held on July 4, that being, with all the modern appliances of war deployed into the fray, and the battle charge fought as it would have been fought as per 1922-style.[43]

The signal corps went to work laying down wire for communications and the fighters and scouts took to the air to reconnoiter the battleground. The tanks were not deployed, for whatever reason, so Marines representing tanks were dispersed and given certain flags to carry to represent where the tanks would be and their planned movements. "Several companies of Machine Gunners, with all their field paraphernalia established machine gun pits on favorable ground and simulated automatic fire," *The Gettysburg Times* reported.[44]

But once again, rain brought activities to a halt. *The Gettysburg Times* reported, "Rain again interfered with the night program, Thursday evening, when a heavy shower passed over Camp Harding shortly after 8 o'clock and put an end to all activities…the movie program had just gotten underway when the rain began to fall and everyone hurried to shelter."[45]

The downpour "…played some havoc in

Major General John Lejeune greets a soldier (center right) at Camp Harding.

**"The Marines traveled in hard luck during their stay at Gettysburg. They either concluded they could not go on exhibition without plenty of their natural element and arranged with the weather bureau for plenty of rain, or that bureau has some grievance against the Marines, for they were simply deluged with rain…and when it did rain, it poured…"**

*- Gettysburg Compiler*, **July 8, 1922.**[46]

William Sproul, Warren Harding and Elbert Lee Trinkle in front of the Canvas White House.

camp...Drains about the tents became blocked and in some cases the tents were flooded, while in the case of several soldiers, the high wind proved too strong and the tents were blown over," the newspaper reported. Weather would continue to be a factor throughout the event.[47]

"It has rained at intervals for two days now, and tonight the sky is black with promise of more rain tomorrow." *The Sun* reported. "All the marine hopes is that it doesn't blow hard enough to wreck the cooks' tents."[48]

**Battle for Herr Ridge**

For a rather amazing, and no doubt one of the most spectacular, pre-July 1 maneuvers of some size, it appears that the local *The Star and Sentinel* had the most in-depth report of it, while *The Gettysburg Times* had very little, and, surprisingly, *The Sun* and *The Washington Post*, who had covered the event rather thoroughly, appears to have had nothing.

The Marines were scrambled sometime before 11 a.m. on the morning of July 29 for another impromptu call-to-arms when orders were passed down indicating that "flank and advance guard (of the enemy) had seized Seminary Ridge from the Chambersburg road to the sharp bend in West Confederate avenue," *The Star and Sentinel* reported. "Units from the Sixth and Tenth Regiments were ordered at 11 o'clock to attack and seize promptly McPherson Ridge from the Chambersburg 'pike to the knoll one mile southeast of the Fairplay school house."[49]

As the "enemy" was driven off McPherson Ridge, they fell back "to the West of Willoughby Run" and established a defensive position along Herr Ridge. "His (the enemy's) main force, about one infantry regiment and a battery of 75's (75mm cannon), prepared to defend a position on Herr Ridge, on a front of 2,000 yards, south of the Chambersburg road," *The Star and Sentinel* reported. Aircraft was deployed to act as scout and conduct reconnaissance, patrolling the enemy-occupied territory between Herr Ridge and Cashtown.[50]

That this was to be a hold-nothing-back exercise was reflected in the details of the unfolding engagement in the newspaper. "The attacking forces are accompanied with all auxiliary arms, field rations for one day, being maintained at all rail heads. The Marine Quartermaster Corps have been

Smedley Butler, President Warren Harding, John J. Pershing, and John Archer Lejeune in front of Canvas White House.

# PLAY BALL!

General Smedley D. Butler umpiring for the Philadelphia Police Baseball Game circa 1925. Smedley had taken leave of absence from the Marines at the time, and was serving as the Philadelphia director of Public Safety in 1924 and 1925.

A good many of the Marines managed to find time during the day on June 28 to engage in a baseball game with a local Maryland baseball team, or just to enjoy watching the game. The Marine team had challenged the Emmitsburg, Md., players to a game while passing through the town on June 26.

The coming challenge-game, to take place at "firemen's field," was a big deal to Emmitsburg residents in a town that *The Frederick Post* described as a town that "begins and ends at an attractive fountain in the principle square." The newspaper also reported, "Michael Hoke, the Civil War veteran, who runs a 'near-beer place'…has ordered up cases and cases of 'prohibition beverages,' which he promises he will give away to his leathernecks, whether they beat his home-town team or not."[51]

"This afternoon (June 28)," *The Gettysburg Times* reported, "every available truck and machine in the camp was commandeered to transport the sea soldiers to Emmitsburg...Two bands from the local camp were taken along to furnish music during the game."[52]

"On Wednesday afternoon, when the marine baseball team played an exhibition game with a team from that place, they were royally entertained by the people of the Maryland town," *The Gettysburg Times* reported. "The ladies of Emmitsburg made a great quantity of cake and candy which was served to the Marines during the game, together with ice cream and soda."[53]

"It is said that the entire population of the town attended the game, as a half-holiday had been declared by the business men," the newspaper wrote.[54]

The Marines didn't show Emmitsburg much mercy. *The Frederick Post* reported the Marines beat the Emmitsburg team 13-1. *The Washington Post* reported that the score had been 14-1.[55]

"But the Marylanders took the beating like sportsmen and their townfolk returned it to the sea soldiers with quantities of cake and fudge prepared by the good women of Emmitsburg." *The Washington Post* reported.[56]

Likewise, the Marines' baseball team "whitewashed" an opposing team from the American Chain Company, of York, in a game held June 30 on the grounds of the Gettysburg College according to *The Frederick Post*. A spectator crowd of hundreds watched the Marines trounce the York company team 16-0.[57]

*The Gettysburg Times* also reported the Marines played a game against the "Gettysburg Ward League" on the same day at 3:30 p.m. at Nixon Field at Gettysburg College (*Editor's Note: Nixon Field was then located at what is now the site of the Musselman Library at the college*).[58]

ordered out as a salvage squad, assisted by the Engineers. The Sanitary Inspector will attend to the proper burial of all 'casualties' while two Chaplains are detailed to look after the burial and keep records of the men killed."[59]

A battalion of Marines of the Fifth Regiment were posted in the area of Lincoln Square to serve as reinforcements. Radios were deployed and telephone lines laid by the signal corps to allow all of the units to stay in touch with the command, the various other units involved, and even the airplanes overhead. Even the "big ears" were brought out and set up to monitor the sky for any sign of enemy airplanes.[60]

As the attacking force prepared to launch the final assault against the defenders of Herr Ridge, a heavy storm descended on the Gettysburg area, ending the ongoing maneuvers and drenching the troops, *The Gettysburg Times* wrote. The aerial night battle that had been canceled on June 28 and rescheduled for June 29 was canceled again.[61]

June 30 - This was the last day that the more than 5,000 Marines would have to themselves, as such, until the public reenactments would commence. The fight for Herr Ridge continued, if on a bit soggier terrain than that of the day before.

However, had it not been for a passing comment in the June 30 edition of *The Gettysburg Times* - "Maneuvers were continued at Camp Harding this morning and enlarged to such an extent, that the battalions engaged covered about sixteen miles of territory during the 'engagement,' which is continuing the attacks on the 'enemy' who was driven back from McPherson Ridge to Willoughby Run (on June 29)" – one might not have even known of this maneuver *en masse,* had it not been for the *Star and Sentinel*.[62]

Aside from concluding the fight for Herr Ridge, the commanders at the encampment managed to inject a few more rehearsals of the charge into an otherwise busy schedule of finishing-up the final touches to the camp and arrangements preparatory to the presidential visit, along with dozens of federal and states dignitaries and foreign dignitaries and emissaries, not to mention tens of thousands of spectators.

Ultimately, a stillness fell over the encampment as the night wore on, and groups of late-night holdouts among the Marines slowly gave into the body's need for rest.

*The Sun* wrote, "Tonight the men in khaki sleep on their arms and wait for the battle tomorrow here, where two great armies fought the greatest battle that ever drenched American soil 59 years ago. They are the United States Marines, ready to give the nation a living picture of the last desperate blow launched by the Confederate States of America."[63]

# HOOCH,

With more than 5,000 Marines ascending upon their "canvas city" on the Codori Farm, it was only a matter of time before those seeking to gain illicit profit appeared on the scene.

The first of these "vices" to make its presence known was the arrival of the bootleggers, but the prostitution and gamblers would soon follow. State police terminated an effort by several individuals to peddle "bootlegged" liquor to the Marines and spectators during the Fourth of July weekend.

"A week-end effort on the part of the State Police to check the flood of liquor being poured into Gettysburg for sale to Marines and civilians alike, netted three arrests with more expected," *The Gettysburg Times* reported. Arrested were John Brown and Harry Tate, both of Gettysburg, and Fred Saum, Fairfield. Brown was arrested Saturday, July 1, Saum was arrested Sunday, July 2, and Tate was arrested Monday, July 3. Police reported that the trio were selling gin at $8.00 a quart and corn whiskey at $4.00 per pint.[64]

Next came the prostitutes. "Another species of lawlessness was nipped in the bud early," the Gettysburg Compiler reported. "State Police in plain clothes were approached and solicited by the harlot and in short order a number were under arrest and locked up and had to submit to tests (for sexually transmittable diseases)…"[65]

The Star and Sentinel (Gettysburg) stated, "State Police are continuing their drive against alleged immoral women, who have followed the Marines to their encampment here. Tuesday, they arrested Mrs. Helen Deporter and Miss Edith Campbell, both of Washington, on Centre Square (Lincoln Square), as they were in the act of soliciting among the soldiers.[66]

The state troopers then began dealing with issues that seemed to have been occurring within the bounds of the Lew Dufour Carnival, which was making a two-week appearance from June 26 through July 8, in Gettysburg under the auspices of the Albert J. Lentz American Legion. The carnival had set-up on vacant ground along Steinwehr Avenue, located approximately where the Heritage Museum is presently located, up to perhaps as far as where American Fuel service station is presently located.[67]

Photograph of the area in which the Lew Dufour Carnival was set-up in June and July, 1922, the lot along on Steinwehr Avenue having been vacant at the time.

# HOOKERS, AND HIGH STAKES

The carnival had already escaped near-disaster on June 26 when a Marine de Havilland DH-4B bomber crashed within 20 feet of some of the carnival tents, killing both aviators who were aboard (see Chapter Four: Knights of the Air).

Of particular interest to state police was a "sideshow" called the "Hawaiian," because of "its alleged indecent character."[68]

All of the suspects detained by state police "were members of the Hawaiian troup (which) were arrested last Saturday evening, when state police…raided their attraction because of its alleged indecent character…The indecent remarks of the girls connected with the show while performing before the crowd outside their tent caused police to place the 'Hawaiian' under ban. Inside, the show was declared not fit for women and children to attend."[69]

The female suspects taken into custody included: Marie Billard, 21, Washington, D.C.; Betty Young, 23, Hagerstown, Md.; Mildred Zantour, 35, Raleigh, N. C.; and May Winfield, 25, Raleigh, N. C. Only one male was arrested, that being Edwin Deford, 30, Baltimore. *The Gettysburg Times* reported that Deford was determined to be suffering from a "virulent venereal disease," and was to

be transported to a state hospital "until this condition improved." The four females "were lodged in the local jail, and blood tests taken Monday (July 2) at the Warner Hospital," the samples then having to be sent to Baltimore for analysis.[70]

Of course, those involved in gambling could also not resist an easy profit. A detail of state policemen under command of Captain Wilson C. Price visited the carnival grounds and closed four wheels of chance..." "The wheels were said by the police to be gambling devices of the rankest kind. Some of the fakers in charge of the wheels were also said by the police to be short-changing their customers," the newspaper reported. "Other wheels were not giving awards on every spin, thereby placing them in a class of gambling devices which are under ban."[71]

The carnival apparently took subsequent steps to ensure that there was no replay of the prostitution issue when they moved on to York. "The closest approach to this kind of performance" *The Gettysburg Times* wrote, "was 'Mamie, the Fattest Girl,' said to weigh over 600 pounds, and 'Minnie Wa Wa,' another girl in the snake snow," although there were some games of chance closed down by law enforcement during the York carnival.[72]

"Cemetery Ridge fell today, the blazing hills and knolls that hurled back the Confederate Army's massed attacks in 1863 were silenced this morning by the United States marines, sneaking like Indians among the wheat shocks and through the stubble and oat fields, while big guns pounded to pulp and machine guns peppered to death the fortresses that had held the old Union Army safe 59 years ago."

The (Baltimore) Sun,
July 5, 1922[1]

# CHAPTER 6

# PICKETT'S CHARGE

*"Even now I can hear them cheering as I gave the order, 'Forward!' I can feel the thrill of their joyous voices as they called out all along the line, 'We'll follow you, Marse George. We'll follow you—we'll follow you.' Oh, how faithfully they kept their word—following me on—on—to their death, and I, believing in the promised support, led them on—on—on—Oh, God!"*

– Confederate General George Picket, July 6, 1863.[2]

**Delegation of command**

The first day of the three-day presentation of Pickett's Charge, July 1, opened with torrential rain and thunderstorms, which subsequently transformed, by early afternoon, into "oppressive heat" - the "oppressive heat" being rather something of a trademark in weather for June and July in Gettysburg...more often than not. But by the time the troops began forming-up for the reenactment, the rains had passed, leaving the encampments "covered by mud," as *The Gettysburg Times* described it.[3]

Sometime during July 30 and the morning of July 1, it was announced that Confederate General

**Pages 118-119:** Marines begin to fall as the battle to capture the Codori house and farmstead gets underway. **Page 120 Top:** Marines reenact Pickett's Charge using flags to help spectators identify which Confederate units are being represented. **Page 120 Bottom:** Theodore Roosevelt, Jr. and John Archer Lejeune, center. **Above:** "Wounded" Marine lies on the battlefield during one of the Pickett's Charge reenactments.

Robert E. Lee was to be portrayed by Colonel Frederick L. Bradman, commander of the Marines Fourth Brigade, during the several reenactments of Pickett's Charge, and Major H.B. Pratt would portray Confederate General James Longstreet. Bradman observed the charges from the site of the Virginia monument, while Pratt stood-by at the crest of Seminary Ridge behind the Canvas White House.[4]

The part of Confederate General George Pickett was portrayed by Colonel James K Tracey, regimental commander of the Fifth Marines, his adjutant being portrayed by Captain LeRoy P. Hunt, while Confederate General Lewis Armistead was portrayed by Major William P. Upshur.[5]

*The (Hanover) Evening Sun* reported that Lieutenant Colonel Chandler Campbell (*Editor's Note: The newspaper misidentified the officer as "Lieutenant Colonel Chandler"*), in command of the Tenth Regiment Field Artillery, portrayed Confederate Colonel Edward Porter Alexander, the young artilleryman who was placed in command of the 140 Confederate cannon which opened fire on the Union lines at the commencement of the 1863 charge. Additionally, the newspaper also reported that other Confederate generals were portrayed by: Major C.H. Wills, portraying General James L. Kemper; Major Thomas Barber, portraying General Richard B. Garnett; Major Chester L. Gawne, portraying General Alfred Scales; Major C.D. Matthews, portraying General Isaac Trimble; Major Howard Parsons, portraying General Joseph R. Davis; and Major E. H. Moore, portraying General

**Left:** President Harding watches the Marines reenact Pickett's Charge at Gettysburg. **Below:** Harding leaving for Gettysburg on July 1

James J. Archer.[6]

Beets were distributed among the troops to simulate blood during the battle, the beets having been supplied by the quartermaster, a half bushel to each regiment, which were then "cut up and boiled," the juice then being retained for the simulation of blood. The troops were also issued bandages to apply to the "wounds" as well, *The Sun* reported.[7]

## The president arrives

Having reviewed the troops at the White House in Washington, D.C. a week and a half earlier, the Marines invited the president to be their guest on the battlefield at Gettysburg as he had done on the battlefield at the Wilderness the previous year.

President Warren G. Harding and his entourage of more than 40 members of his staff, Secret Service, and select reporters, left Washington shortly after noon on Saturday, July 1.[8] For the Hardings, it was the beginning of a week-long vacation.

Maryland State Police were waiting at the district line to escort the president's part through the state.[9] They traveled on much of the same route that the Marines had taken, following the Rockville Pike. However, the president's group of eight cars[10] quickly passed over the countryside in roughly three-and-a-half hours.

Among the presidential party were the First Lady Florence Harding, General John "Blackjack" Pershing, Charles G. Dawes who was the retiring director of the budget, Brigadier General Charles Sawyer who served as the president's personal physician, and the president's personal secretary, George Christian. The party arrived in Frederick, Md., sometime after 2:15 p.m. "His arrival was heralded by the ringing of bells, and the playing of patriotic airs on the town chimes," *The (Frederick)*

Marines portraying Confederate soldiers reenact the penetration of the High Water Mark. Probably photographed on July 1 or July 3, 1922.

*News* reported.[11] Just as they had for the Marines the Saturday before, residents of Frederick lined the streets to watch the president's arrival. The crowd cheered him and he waved to the watchers from his car.

Gen. Pershing was also recognized among the passengers in the cars. The crowd cheered him as well and he waved back to them.[12] Although the president did not stop in the city, he did make a brief stop at the Richfield Farm about three miles north of Frederick.[13]

The late Admiral Winfield Scott Schley had been born on that farm. Schley was known as the "Hero of Santiago" for his fighting during the Spanish-American War in 1898. "Commanding the 'flying squadron,' Schley, in the absence of his superior officer, impetuously took direct command of the fleet and destroyed Admiral Cervera's Spanish squadron in the harbor of Santiago on July 3, 1898. As a result,

the war was nearly won and Schley was advanced to the rank of rear admiral," Cathy Hunter wrote in *National Geographic*.[14]

Frederick City officials and others were on hand at the farm to greet the group. Anne Schley, a relative of the admiral's, presented the president and Pershing a bouquet of flowers.[15] A 40-foot-tall flag pole and marker had been placed near the driveway to mark the importance of the home.

After the stop, the party traveled north through Thurmont and Emmitsburg as the Marines had the week before. The Marines had had hot weather, though. The president's party ran into a rainstorm that turned the roads into treacherous passage.

As the caravan approached the state line, it slowed to a stop in order for governors William Sproul of Pennsylvania, Albert Ritchie of Maryland, and Lee Trinkle of Virginia to greet the presi-

**Below: From left to right:** Pennsylvania Governor William Sproul, General John J. Pershing, First Lady Florence Harding (in white) President Warren Harding and Governor Elbert Lee Trinkle in front of the Canvas White House. The other two women are unidentified. **Pages 126-127:** Batteries of 75mm guns and mortars deployed along a portion of Seminary Ridge commence firing at the beginning of one of the reenactments of Pickett's Charge. Photographed either July 1, July 3, or July 4, 1922.

> **"The strangest thing about them was they moved without seeming to move. No motion of their legs or bodies could be detected from the old Union lines. They seemed to be rolling across like figures on an escalator, as though the ground itself was bearing them forward while they stood still. And there were so many of them...like parading battalions of ghosts."**
>
> - *The Baltimore Sun*, July 2, 1922.[16]

dent. The car carrying Gen. Sawyer, his wife, Dawes, and his wife couldn't stop in time. The car swerved off the road to avoid a collision. Instead, it went into a ditch and his a fence. No one was injured and the car was pushed back onto the road undamaged.[17]

Pennsylvania State Police took over for the Maryland State Police at the Mason-Dixon Line[18] and escorted the group to Camp Harding and the Canvas White House, arriving around 3:55 p.m. on July 1.[19] When they arrived at Camp Harding, Marines, standing at attention, lined the pathways of the encampment.

As the president and his entourage arrived at the front of the Canvas White House, the artillery provided a 21-gun salute.[20] The president inspected the camp with Brigadier General Smedley Butler and then returned to the Canvas White House to prepare to watch the Pickett's Charge re-enactment, which began at 5 p.m. The group watched from a vantage point in an observation tower erected on Cemetery Ridge in order to get the full sweep of the historical re-enactment that lasted less than an hour.

Following the excitement of the afternoon, the president and his party were guests as a dinner in their honor in the Marine camp.

As the presidential party settled into their sumptuous overnight camp, the first lady had help with putting the Canvas White House in order. Being the various Marine officers and dignitaries at the compound were waiting to greet the president, his wife was introduced to several local volunteers who offered to assist the first lady during her stay, which included

Gettysburg College President William Anthony Granville's wife, Ida Adelia Irwin Granville, Ruth V. Stallsmith, Evelyn Toot, Madeline Roth, and Constance Weaver.[21]

Harding and his accompanying compatriots, who had spent a short time posing for group photographs on the steps of the Canvas White House, made their way to the Ziegler Grove observation tower. The group included the president, the first lady, Gen. Pershing, Gov. Sproul, Gov. Trinkle, Acting Secretary of the Navy Theodore Roosevelt, Jr., U.S. Senator George Wharton Pepper (Pa.), Commandant of the Marine Corps Major General John A. Lejeune, Major General Wendell C. Neville, Brig. Gen.1 Butler, Dawes, Dr. Sawyer and his wife May, Christian, U.S. Senator Joseph Medill McCormick (Ill.), Speaker of the House Frederick H. Gillett, and others.[22]

Colonel E.B. Cope, superintendent of the Gettysburg National Military Park, stood near the base of the tower. Cope had actually been present at the July 3, 1863, charge, as a result of his having served as a sergeant in the topographical engineers attached to Union General George Meade's headquarters at the time. Meade, of course, commanded the Union troops at the Battle of Gettysburg.[23]

*The Gettysburg Times* noted that not all of the presidential entourage and accompanists climbed to the top of the tower, and that a number of the ladies, including Florence Harding and state governor's wife, Charlotte, "went about half way up in the tall steel structure, from where they viewed the staging

of the big event with much interest."[24]

## The battle is joined

As the time of battle approached, it has been estimated that as many as a hundred thousand spectators had already descended upon the scene, or were continuing to do so. *The Star and Sentinel* reported that, "For miles on the front and either flank of the territory over which the charge was made, as well as from other points of vantage, including the Round Tops, a great throng of people, who motored here from nearby sections of the country, witnessed the pageant."[25]

At around 5 p.m., smoke "candles" *(Editor's Note: Probably what was also sometimes referred to as smoke pots.)* were set-off south of the reenactment site, the smoke being add ed to "set the stage" before the attack commenced. The smoke screen thus launched was apparently intended to also be a signal for the Confederate artillery barrage to begin.

Suddenly, two of the Confederate 75mm guns fired, the signal for Lt. Campbell to direct the commencement of the opening barrage of the artillery that he had ordered "concealed" in an artillery park on Seminary Ridge (A number of the 75mm guns were also placed along Cemetery Ridge and around Little Round Top to represent the federal artillery), George M. Chandler wrote in the July 1922 *Infantry Journal*.[26]

It can be somewhat difficult to follow Chandler's time-line in his account, so it has been presumed from his account that the two-gun signal he mentioned, preceded the charge of July 1. *The Sun* mentioned a single artillery shot being fired, as a rolling smoke screen crossed the fields.

"At 5 o'clock little clouds of white smoke jetted up from the ground under the far off trees," *The*

Marines portraying Confederate soldiers reenact the penetration of the High Water Mark. Probably photographed on

> "Astonishment was expressed by members of the president's party, which included General Pershing, General Dawes and General Sawyer, that such a manner of fighting could have been practiced in the civil war. They contended the withering concentration of gun fire executed in modern warfare would have annihilated the whole brigade. If was said a single modern machine gun could have stopped the charge."
>
> - The Canton Daily News, July 5, 1922[27]

*Baltimore Sun* wrote. "Off to the left they started first, then spread out toward the west in a solid white line, until the line seemed lost in the distance. It grew thicker and thicker, rising until it hid the trees. Suddenly red flashes split through the white wall, and next second the boom of a gun rolled across the mountain."[28]

The guns were then rolled forward by hand from the artillery park behind Seminary Ridge until they were standing hub-to-hub, alongside of the period smoothbore guns of the Confederate Army, on West Confederate Avenue. This placed them about 1,400 yards from their intended targets on Cemetery Ridge. When the artillery received the cannons to commence fire, "the recoil of the 75mm guns shook the earth," *The Gettysburg Times* wrote.[29]

Chandler wrote that the 75mm howitzers also used black powder rounds in the guns to add to the effect of "fog of war" on the field, and to provide an authentic appearance to the battle reenactment.[30]

Campbell's opening barrage represented a 30-minute version of the 1863 duel in which Confederate Col. Alexander, commanding Gen. Longstreet's reserve artillery, was ordered to direct the opening of a two-hour barrage of 140 Confederate cannon aimed primarily at the center of the Union line on Cemetery Ridge, as a prelude to Pickett's Charge.

"Faster and faster the flashes of red came through and quicker and quicker the artillery thunder rolled over the fields, until it sounded like the beating of drums… Guns roared both ways across the field now. Puffs of smoke leaped out from the Round Tops on the left of the Union Line and from Cemetery Hill on the right. The flashes along Seminary Ridge persisted...," *The Sun* reported.[31]

*The Evening Sun* reported that the 21-gun artillery salute fired upon the arrival of the president, and the subsequent artillery barrage that preceded the charge, could be "plainly heard" in Hanover, some 13 miles away. The newspaper stated "… many people believed at first that the sound was that of distant thunder. To the older residents of the town the days of the battle of Gettysburg were vividly recalled."[32]

When the half-hour barrage subsided, the Marines representing the Southern advance began, preceded by a skirmish line of sharpshooters, who were deployed about "twenty paces" in front of the battle line. The advancing Confederates bore flags that were marked in such a manner that the spectators could ascertain whose troops they were representing that had taken place in the original engagement 59 years prior.

In order to aid spectators in keeping track of the units on the field, the Confederate regiments carried white and red Army signal flags as their respective battle flags, while the names of the generals who were represented in the charge were written in white on blue cloth.[33]

On July 4 the Marines will fight the Battle of Gettysburg as they think it ought to have been fought – with tanks, airplanes, observation balloons and machine guns. They don't need any rehearsal for this. They learned a good deal about it in France."

– *The (Baltimore) Sun*

June 28, 1922[34]

**Page 130 Top:** Marine skirmishes begin to pave the way for a general assault across Emmitsburg Road. **Page 130 Bottom:** Machine gunners fire toward the enemy from the fence line in front of the Codori house around the time the battle was declared a Confederate victory. Photographed on July 3. **Above:** Marine machine gun crews set-up along Emmitsbrg Road after Union troops relinquished control of the immediate vicinity following their retreat from the Codori farmstead. **Pages 132-133:** Marines fall back toward Emmitsburg Road following the collapse of Pickett's Charge. Probably photographed on July 1 or July 3, 1922.

At first, there was so much smoke on the field from the smoke candles and the artillery rapidly firing black powder-filled rounds into the air, that the advancing Confederate battle line was not easily discerned, but when they were spotted in the haze, some said it appeared the ghosts of soldiers past were returned out of time itself and onto the battlefield.

Writing about the ensuing fight, the *New York Tribune* wrote, "Then they began to move forward...and for the watchers there was a thrill as though the ghosts of Pickett's men were massed once more for another try for victory...there were six lines of men stretching along a mile front."[35]

Even *The Gettysburg Times* noted, "In spectre (*sic*) like form, it seemed, as the figures were dimly outlined through the dense smoke of battle, that the soldiers of the Confederacy had actually come back and were reenacting that charge which proved fatal to the cause of the Southern States."[36]

The Confederate Marines advanced shoulder-to-shoulder, nineteenth-century style, until they reached the Emmitsburg Road, where they were confronted with surmounting the fencing that represented the last obstacle in their path to the High Water Mark.

*The Sun* recorded, "Now the crackling of rifles was a steady chorus, and the ('battalions of ghosts') were plainly living figures. They fell upon the fence in clouds, like mobs of insects alighting, firing furiously. Some toppled over the fence, fell headlong in the road and lay there. Some went suddenly limp across the top rail and hung like clothes drying in the sun. But the mass of them went over, crossed the road, climbed the next fence and were at the foot of the knoll."[37]

Some of the advancing troops had also been provided with shotguns loaded with black powder rounds that they would fire towards the ground, as the troops progressed in order to simulate artillery shell explosions. The Marines in the vicinity of the "explosions" would then fall "dead" or "wounded" around the detonation thus produced.[38]

Standing at the base of the Ziegler's Grove tower, Park Superintendent Cope, emotionally caught up in the moment that he had once lived through,

Marine attends "wounded" as the troops begin to fall back from the area of the High Water Mark toward Emmitsburg Road. Probably photographed on July 1 or July 3, 1922.

mounted the first step of the tower and yelled at the advancing Confederates, "Get back there, you Rebs!"[39]

The Marines, having crossed the Emmitsburg Road, continued on toward the stone wall that comprised the high water mark of the Battle of Gettysburg, at the crest of Cemetery Ridge, but not before a portion of the advancing Marines charged the Codori homestead on the east side of the road, routing an army of chickens – literally, in this case – in the process. "Chickens on the farm, terrified by the sudden appearance of these khaki-clad figures and heavy rifle fire, flew in all directions for safety," *The (Gettysburg) Star and Sentinel* reported.[40]

At 5:20 p.m., the climactic storming of "the angle" began, led by Upshur, (portraying General Armistead). Upshur's father had been wounded in the service of the Confederate States during the actual war, while Upshur himself had become a Medal of Honor recipient for his actions in 1915 in Haiti.

As the final moments approached, *The Sun* reported, "The din of firing was fearful. From the far-off woods on Seminary ridge the cannonade had almost ceased, but from all around…the Union guns now roared a thunderous chorus. Then came the 'rebel yell' and the last rush. They were at the stone fence, in a yelling, shooting mass. The Confederates were at the Bloody Angle again."[41]

Upshur placed his hat on his sword, and then led his Marines over the wall, and was subsequently "mortally wounded," falling beside one of Union guns in the battery at a crucial angle in the Union defense.

The collision of the Confederate Marines with those representing the Union seemed so realistic that those observing the attack from immediately behind the Union line began to retreat, themselves. "As the attackers crossed the wall with all the enthusiasm and fury of real battle, the crowds of people who lined Hancock avenue, to view the event, instinctively fell back as before a real foe," *The Star and Sentinel* reported.[42]

The charge, having reached the maximum point of penetration of the Union line, had ended, and the hundreds of wounded Confederates began to make their way across the fields, they had previously charged across, to assail the enemy position on Cemetery Ridge.

"A shivering yellow pup, with tail tucked into its dragging belly, crept to the side of one of the fallen marines who lay spraddled out with his closed eyes to the sun," the *New York Tribune* reported. "The pup licked his face sympathetically once, twice, then the stricken 'Confederate' leaped to his feet and rejoined his fighting but now retreating comrades."[43]

Then the fields suddenly fell silent as "a bugle was sounded from the High Water Mark, which called the 'dead' and 'wounded' to arise… (followed by) loud applause, from all sections of the large fields, greeted this 'awakening' of the dead.'"[44]

As the president and his entourage prepared to descend the tower in Ziegler's Grove, a rumor was quickly spread that he was to give a speech, and a multitude of spectators gathered at the base as he and his compatriots climbed down, but there was no intended speech, although the president did shake quite a number of hands in the process of exiting the immediate area.[45]

Harding then made his way over to the Canvas White House, and would then spend the only night he would spend in the structure that had required so many man-hours to create. The compound, however, would not go unused, because it continued to house guests and dignitaries up through the end of July 4.

The president did have dinner that evening with the officers of the sea soldiers in the main mess tent. "A table on a raised platform, had been constructed at the end of the regular mess table, for the President and his party." Governor Sproul, who had arrived at the site earlier than the president, enjoyed lunch at the setup, with a dozen Civil War veterans as his guests.[46]

A thunderstorm encroaching upon the area around 9 p.m. grounded the planes of the Marine First Aviation Group, and an aerial attack that had been planned was cancelled, although the Marines

*"Seminary Ridge, the old Confederate line, looked as peaceful as a long grove of trees can look under the sun of a July afternoon. In front of the trees lay the Marine camp. The huge round back of a captive balloon, inflated but still lashed to the ground, lay shining like a giant hippopotamus"*

- The *Baltimore Sun, July 2, 1922*[49]

**Above:** Dignitary speaking during to group of people at Camp Harding, captioned by Library of Congress as "Senator George Wharton Pepper(?)".

did scan the sky with searchlights and demonstrated anti-aircraft fire for whomever remained onsite in the way of interested parties ahead of the storm.[47]

In spite of the general saturation of the encampment, the president began the morning of July 2 by having breakfast at the Marine mess tent. The *Washington Post* reported that the president "was in rare good humor when the breakfast hour came, and paid no attention to the muddy condition of the street leading from his quarters to the tent where the meal was served."[48]

Following breakfast, the president and his party attended Sunday services at 8:30 a.m. held by Episcopalian minister Chaplain Edwin B. Niver, assisted by Bishop James D. Darlington, of the Harrisburg diocese, in front of the "Canvas White House." Senator Pepper read from the eighth chapter of Matthew regarding the story of the centurion. The president declined being seated

and stood with the Marines attending the service.[50]

As the president and some members of his party were preparing to depart the camp, the presidential vehicles were found as having become stuck in the mud, and had to be extracted with the help of the Marines. "The severe storm of last night left the parade grounds a sea of mud, and when the presidential party left the field for Uniontown the machines used in the journey had to be hauled to Confederate avenue by army trucks."[51]

As had been the case when Harding had arrived at the camp the day before, "A salute of twenty one guns was given the president as he left the camp," *The Gettysburg Times reported.*[52]

By 9:30 a.m., the president and his party drove west along the Lincoln Highway, heading for Marion, Ohio, the president's hometown. He would spend the next few days there celebrating the town's centennial anniversary.

## Camp turned bog

The Marine camp had come under a seemingly endless siege, not from a hail of gunfire, but rather from deluge of rain and wind.

As many a modern Civil War reenactor could readily testify, when the annual Gettysburg reenactment and weather conspire, the event can quickly degrade into a "mud march," and the troops and sutlers involved can be observed loading their soaking wet canvas into, or onto, their vehicle and trailers, following the event, which then have to generally be completely reassembled when they return home in order to facilitate drying all the canvas before mildew or mold can become established.

The storm that grounded the airplanes late Saturday evening was described as one of the worst of the several that had deluged the site since the encampment had been initially established on June 26.

Fortunately, Sunday had been set aside for the Marines as a day of rest, and provided a break from reenacting and maneuvers. It also provided a day to attempt drying out their belongings and equipment that had become even more saturated overnight.

*The Frederick Post* reported, regarding the overnight storm, "The Marine camp here may be afloat by morning. A heavy rain, which has been falling for about four hours, has so flooded the encampment that the Marines will probably have to swim out of their 'pup' tents to answer the reveille call. At present Camp Harding has been divided into two sections by a swelling creek...The whole Fourth Brigade is literally marooned, and if the steady downfall keeps up all night they will have to depict Pickett's Charge tomorrow in bathing suits"[53]

Periodic rains over the course of the previous days had saturated the camp and fields, even prompting the command to consider possibly ordering the troops home a day early, breaking camp after the Fourth of July charge "It is altogether likely, that should more rain fall, the Marines will break camp on Wednesday and start on their return hike to Quantico, a day before schedule...The ground has been soaked to such a depth by the frequent rains that the heavy trucks sink to the axel in the mud, while automobiles are stalled in all parts of the camp," *The Star and Sentinel reported.*[54]

The Marines fared no better overnight from Sunday into Monday. *The Gettysburg Times* described what awaited the Marines as they awoke in camp on July 3. "Wading about in the mud and water, which covered Camp Harding, this morning, the Marines were busily engaged in drying out their soaked equipment and trying to drain the water from the pools standing in the tents..."[55]

*Leatherneck Magazine* wrote, "It is reported that it rained while the Marines were at Camp Harding! It may be added that the report was not exaggerated. It did. If spectators wanted to know why Marines are called 'soldiers of the sea' all they had to do was to look around and watch the sea run down the company streets, and alas, through some of the tents."[56]

## "Pickett's ducks" charge again

Two of the noteworthy guests with direct, or

Helen Dortch Longstreet.

137

A View of Pickett's Charge as presented by the Marines. Courtesy of the U.S. Marine Corps Historical Company.

semi-direct, ties to the conflict of 1863 included Helen Dortch Longstreet, widow of Confederate Gen. Longstreet, the officer who was in overall command of the charge at Gettysburg during the war, and Gen. Pickett's grandson, George F. Pickett, III.

Longstreet viewed the charge in the company of General Lejeune from the observation tower in Ziegler's Grove, as the president and his entourage had done two days prior.

July 3 represented the actual date the ill-fated charge took place 59 years prior, with at least one outstandingly notable difference. "Today a Pickett saw the charge from the Union side of the battlefield," *The Sun* reported. "He stood by the guns that had wrought destruction to his grandsire's hopes and fighting men..."[57]

The *New York Tribune* reported that Gen. Pickett's wife, Lasalle, attended the July 3 event, but the general's grandson told *The Sun* her doctor

wouldn't allow it. It could well have been that General Pickett's wife had attended, but that her grandson had wanted to shield her from all the attention she would have been subjected to.[58]

The attack and repulse was essentially the same as held on July 1 before President Harding. Therefore, repeating it all would be somewhat redundant, although some additional occurrences may be worth noting, for example, this version was done in heavy rains.

"Pickett's charge was less fun for the Marines today than last Saturday, when President Harding saw it," *The Sun* reported. "It soaked 'em to the skin. But a leatherneck can get fun out of anything but a poor dinner, and they took their places in the line shortly before 3 o'clock, quacking like ducks and shouting: Take back these blanks and give us depth charges. Where are the life preservers? I don't need this gun; give me a pair of oars. Don't shoot the enemy; catch 'em with a hook and line."[59]

**"Pickett's ducks quacked as they charged across the bog between Seminary and Cemetery Ridges and 10,000 spectators from all over the country, who stood in the rain on the afternoon of July 3, to watch the great spectacle, mistook the quacks for the rebel yell." - Captain George M. Chandler, "Gettysburg, 1922."**

*- Infantry Journal, July, 1922.*[61]

Marines reenacting Pickett's Charge July 1 or July 2 during which they carried flags to enable spectators to see which units were being portrayed.

# THE BOYS OF '63

*"In great deeds something abides. On great fields something stays. Forms change and pass; bodies disappear; but spirits linger, to consecrate the ground for the vision-place of souls."*
— General Joshua Lawrence Chamberlain, 1889[62]

Any significant battle-related event held on the Gettysburg battlefield served as a powerful magnet for the veterans of the American Civil War, particularly for those who had fought in the 1863 engagement, at least as long as there were any veterans who remained alive.

One veteran of the Civil War who fought at Gettysburg and was "on location" from the start of the Marine expedition from Quanitco, even before that, and that was park Superintendent E.B. Cope, During the Battle of Gettysburg in 1863, he served as a topographical engineer with Union General George Meade's headquarters. In 1922, he was superintendent of the Gettysburg battlefield.[63]

Veterans of the blue and gray began to arriving on June 30. The first on the scene, aside from Cope, was W.A. McAneny, who had served in the Maryland Union cavalry during the war. "He had not fought at Gettysburg," but resided in Gettysburg at the time and was home, absent without leave from "General French's command" at Frederick, after he had allegedly become separated and couldn't relocate his unit. While at home, he learned that the Confederate forces had begun to converge upon his home town.[64]

There seems to be no record of the numbers of the boys of 1863 who attended the reenactments.

Who knows how many of the old veterans came and went unnoticed, not wishing to become part of the events, but only to witness it, and to reflect upon it.

Assistant Secretary of the Navy Theodore Roosevelt, Jr. "had a great time hobnobbing with the Civil War veterans," *The Sun* reported, noting that there was "a score or more" of the old veterans watching Pickett's Charge on July 1.[65]

Two veterans were identified by *The Sun* as being C.E. Didenhover, Eleventh Maryland Volunteer Infantry, and E.F.K. Will, initially with the Seventy-Seventh Pennsylvania Regiment, both of whom, after watching the battle, "sat down to lunch and assaulted the beef stew with teeth that don't leap forward to the charge as they did in '61."[66]

Two others cropped up during the July 3 reenactment of Pickett's Charge. They were Private William H. Sayre and Private John Kille, both veterans of the Twelfth New Jersey Volunteers, who had slipped through the security ropes and ended up next to the New Jersey monument, when they asked two nearby "wounded" Marines if they could borrow their guns and shoot.[67]

The leathernecks granted their wish, and handed the old soldiers their rifles and ammunition belts...to the cheering of the crowd behind them. Then they took turns firing at the retreating Confederates.[6]

"All through the crowd...," *The Sun* wrote, "...there were veterans, mostly in blue." Union veteran Captain Robert G. Carter was also watching on July 3. "I wasn't on this exact spot during the charge," he told *The Sun* reporter. "I was up on Little Round Top."[69]

On the evening of July, 4 it was all over. As the Marines marched off, ultimately to fight a different "battle" on a different day at a different battlefield, the veterans of 1863 marched off to become part of a nation's memories.

John Archer Lejeune with a Civil War veteran.

*The Sun* reporter, Raymond S. Tompkins, also observed another difference between Saturday's attack and that of July 3. The Marine causalities had become somewhat selective about where they fell, avoiding mud and attempting to head for grassy areas before collapsing.[60]

General Longstreet's wife wrote, in the July 4 edition of the *New York Tribune,* "I stood to-day in the observation tower on Gettysburg field and saw Longstreet's thin gray lines stretched a mile long across summer wheat fields for the attack on Cemetery Hill…. As the Confederates moved to the thunder of artillery, so realistic was it, the tides of time rolled backward and I stood in the living presence of the South's audacious hope"[70]

The battle, she wrote, "was staged to-day with marvelous accuracy in every detail, exactly as I have heard Gen. Longstreet describe it hundreds of times…. Within the smoke of belching cannon my heart thrilled to the huzzas of the victor and my heart wrestled with the anguish of the vanquished as I saw Dixie's colors go down at Confederate high water mark,"[71]

*The Sun* wrote that the battle reenactment "was a faithful picture," with the exception of the vehicular traffic and that "they were selling ice-cream cones through a window of Meade's headquarters…"[72]

Not to be outdone, the First Aviation Group performed demonstrations of aerial combat at the conclusion of the charge.

According to the *New York Tribune,* 17 aircraft were used in the demonstration. "The first exhibition was a bombing attack in which three huge Martin bombers similar to those which sunk the German battleship Ostfriesland were attacked by two squadrons of fighting planes. The combat planes engaged in aerial warfare, performing loops, spins, Immelman turns *(Editor's Note: Essentially a vertical half-loop, followed by a dive attack),* and all other maneuvers of fighting planes in battle."[73]

## The grand finale

The Fourth of July represented the grand finale, for all intents and purposes, to the more-than-week-long training and battle demonstration campaign around Gettysburg, and the focus of the day's warfare was a presentation of Pickett's Charge as if it had been fought in 1922, and, for a welcoming change, the weather seemed to be predominantly on their side.

The Marines held nothing back in the way of equipment that they had hauled up to the Gettysburg battlefield, including the airplanes and howitzers previously used, as well as hydrogen-filled observation balloons, tanks, machine guns, anti-aircraft guns, "Big Ear" monitoring devices, radio communications, and mortars.

The fury began around 9 a.m., when spectators saw an observation balloon ascend to about 2,000 feet, the balloon hovered above the Marine camp, and representing Confederate observation craft. As soon as the balloons were aloft, their artillery which was posted on Seminary Ridge began to fire, the purpose of the balloons being to ascertain the effect of the rounds being aimed at the enemy positions.[74]

A squadron of four enemy planes, representing Union aircraft, suddenly appeared above Cemetery Ridge to defend the forces located there, and just as quickly, two squadrons of fighters representing the Southern forces rushed up and towards the enemy planes, and were soon engaged in dogfighting, "in which nose dives, spins, loops, Immelman turns and other war maneuvers of fighting aircraft succeeded each other in rapid succession, while bursts of machine gun fire from aloft told when a pilot has succeeded in securing a deadly position on the tail of some other craft," the *New York Tribune* reported.[75]

One of the enemy (Union) planes suddenly broke off and dove at the targeted observation balloon. "Speeding like an angry wasp straight at the big 'sausage,' it veered away and circled the balloon with a 'tat-tat-tat' of machine gun fire. Then it headed back to join its fellows," *The Sun* wrote.[76]

The assault on the balloon was brief, but fatal. Licks of flame appeared, then spread rapidly throughout the craft, which had been inflated with a "half-million cubic feet of hydrogen gas." A dummy, it was generally reported, wearing a parachute was caste forth from the observation basket attached to the underside of the balloon, while a second figure fell to the earth without a chute. As the burning balloon fell to the earth somewhere on the west side of Seminary Ridge, along with the slowly descending "parachutist," the crowd was stunned, some believing that the figures were actually people, and that one of them had fallen to certain death.[77]

*The Sun* reported that, unbeknownst to the many spectators, the fire and the discharge of the occupants of the basket had been controlled from the ground via wires, one of which was electrified to ignite the balloon, or at least so one version goes. *The Sun* also reported that there were two observation balloons aloft, only one of which was sent up to serve as the one slated for destruction.[78]

A second version was reported by the *New York Tribune,* which wrote that the balloon was ignited by "the use of composition bullets, of the kind used in signal pistols, which were burned in the air, being totally consumed in about five hundred feet, yet having hardness enough to penetrate the skin of

*"Behind the ropes, guarded by military policemen, thousands of men and women slowly unclenched their fingers. And the moving picture men still turned their cranks like men gone wild....A score or more of the 'old boys' saw 'Pickett's charge'...Some of them could not speak for minutes after the retreat. They were trembling with excitement; they were living it all over again."*

*– The Baltimore Sun*, **July 2, 1922**[80]

Charles Dawes and U.S. Senator George Wharton Pepper with group touring Camp Harding.

# Thousands view battles

Tens of thousands of spectators arriving by car, bus, and train, converged on the Marine maneuvers, reenactments and encampment during the 10-day stay of the Corps on the Gettysburg battlefield from June 26 through July 5, while attendance was reportedly just shy of what it had been for the 1913 Civil War veterans' reunion.

However, the number of automobiles exceeded that which had been driven to the 1913 reunion, if only because the ownership of vehicles wasn't as prevalent before the 1920s.

Parking arrangements had been worked out to handle the influx of tourists, but these resources would become overwhelmed, and local property owners pitched-in to allow parking for a fee. A great many field parking spaces were rendered useless, however, as the result of nearly daily rain and thunderstorms.

When it came to the use of private property for parking, it became in some instances something of a scam. *The (Frederick) Daily News* reported that some property owners who had charged from 50 cents to a dollar to park on their property, then turned-around and charged the same drivers $3 to $5 to haul the vehicles, which had become stuck in the mud, out of the swamped parking spaces.[81]

It had to have been a grand mess, with all the incoming vehicles and the fields turned into mush, but that didn't deter the tourists who continued to arrive by the tens of thousands. Even ongoing rain didn't deter the masses from coming to see the event, some reportedly stood in ankle-deep water to watch it.

The surge of spectators and tourists was already well under way on June 29, when *The (Baltimore) Sun* recorded, "More visitors swarmed over the camp today than ever before. Truckloads of 'em came from neighboring Maryland and Pennsylvania counties, and the vast parking spaces for automobiles were dotted all day with cars bearing tourist parties."[82]

The first of the Marines' public presentation took place on July 1. *The Sun* stated, "Thousands of people saw it. There is no estimating how many thousands. They were massed in automobiles along the edges of the 'Secor.' They filled the peaks of Round Top and Little Round Top. Along Cemetery Ridge, the objective of the assault, they crowded in many rows, and thousands stood rooted to the ground directly in front of the point of the Confederate wedge…"[83]

The railroads and buses brought all they could handle to the battles as well. "During the forenoon (July 2) regular trains on both the Reading and the Western Maryland lines brought exceptionally large crowds of people," *The Gettysburg Times* reported. "Every bus into Gettysburg was crowded with human freight…"[84]

*The Gettysburg Compiler* reported that there were probably more than 10,000 cars bearing tourists on July 3, while *The Gettysburg Times* reported, "What is expected to be the largest automobile crowd in the history of Gettysburg, began streaming here at daybreak this morning. This influx, it is believed, will continue throughout the day, the peak being reached Tuesday morning."[85]

Regarding the July 4 reenactment, *The Sun* wrote, "The town of Gettysburg looked like the hub of the nation all day, automobiles whose license numbers seemed to bear the names of most of the States in the Union made caravans miles long on every road leading toward the battlefield."[86]

"More than 25,000 people from all parts of the country witnessed both yesterday's old-fashioned battle and today's modern one… Thousands of people swarmed upon the field after the battle, searching for shells and souvenirs," *The Sun* reported.[87]

*The Gettysburg Compiler* estimated that there were between 12,000 and 15,000 cars bearing tourists on July 4, and a crowd of somewhere between 60,000 to 70,000.[88]

*The Washington Post* estimated the crowd viewing the July 4 charged as being 125,000, "whose 15,000 parked cars filled to jamming point every roadway for miles around."[89]

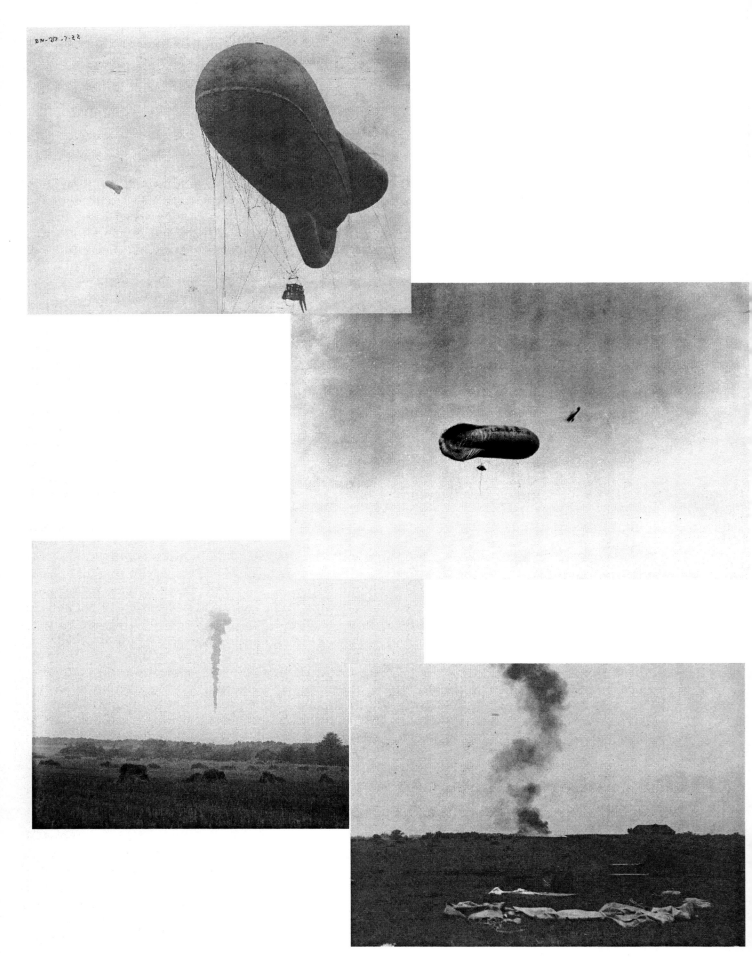

the balloon at short range."[79]

But a third version places a living, and rather daring, Marine in the balloon, who would have been present to ignite the balloon, throw out the dummy without the parachute, then himself parachute to escape. In a poorly written account, the *Rochester and Democrat Observer* wrote "...a thrill was provided when one of the large observation balloons was fired by an attacking airplane and setn (*sic*) flaming to the ground several hundred feet below, after the observer had leaped to safety with a great parachute."[90]

There was no opening artillery barrage as there had been during the beginning of the reenactments on July 1 and 3. This time, the artillery were staged further away, and they fired during the whole charge, with airplanes acting as their spotters. Chandler wrote in *Gettysburg 1922*, "...they (the artillery) were nowhere to be seen, being posted over in the woods 3,000 to 3,500 feet behind the ridge."[91]

Following the initial air action, at around 10:30 a.m., a smokescreen using smoke candles was laid-down on the field in advance of the Confederate advance, and around 10:40 a.m., the Marines began their assault. Unlike the reenactments of July 1 and 3, the Confederates attacked the Union position as they would have done in a "modern" engagement, in squads and platoons, rather than in long shoulder-to-shoulder firing lines.[92]

The Marines advanced across the Codori fields and toward the enemy position on Cemetery Ridge in several waves, each consisting of a line of troops advancing as squads, rather than in battle-line. The idea was to deprive the enemy of a "target-rich environment," or, as *The Sun* put it, "They gave an enemy nothing to hit."[93]

Each wave of squads would advance 20 to 30 feet, and then lay prone, as a second grouping of squads advanced to reinforce them. In this manner, the waves leap-frogged each other towards their objective.[94]

"The machine guns were really there yesterday (July 4). They were firing real bullets. Machine guns can't fire blank ammunition. So were all the other machine guns in the woods on Seminary Ridge. But pits had been dug all around them and the bullets were diving harmlessly into the earth," *The Sun* reported. Further confirming this, The Washington Post noted that "the machine guns used ball ammunition, for machine guns will not function with blank ammunition. The guns were emplaced in previously prepared pits, and the stream of steel-jacketed lead was pumped into the soggy earth."[95]

At some point during the advance, machine gun crews made their way towards Emmitsburg Road, establishing positions along the west side, and eventually, the east side, when help arrived to get them there.

"The audience heard only the thunder of artillery, the ceaseless tat-tat-tat of machine guns and the crack of rifles," *The Sun* reported. "They saw little but puffs of smoke and now and then a few men running, only to disappear suddenly as though the ground had swallowed them...because that is the way men fight in these days."[96]

*The Washington Post* wrote that the engagement so fought readily-established that "a squad of eight men can approximate the fire power of a battalion of the last century," noting, "It became quite apparent to the spectators that modern warfare resolves into movements wherein men fight desperately to

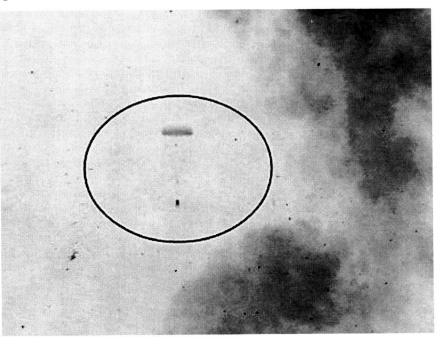

**Page 144:** A series of photos illustrating the balloon attack of July 4. From top to bottom: 1) The two naval observation balloons deployed over Camp Harding during the July 4 battle; 2) DH-4B beginning its attack on an observation balloon, actually photographed during the 1923 New Market maneuvers (A comparable photograph taken at Gettysburg has yet to be found); 3) Burning balloon falling to the ground (see page 143 regarding the parachutist in this photograph); 4) the destroyed balloon lying in a field behind Seminary Ridge. **Right:** Long thought to have been one of two dummies deployed during the July 4 balloon attack, this parachuting figure may have been an actual Marine, who had been on-board the balloon to set the fire, then jump.

kill men they can barely see and are sent to their death by men to whom they are not visible. The inspiring clash of contact combat is a thing of the past."[9]

Little by little, the squads of Marine infantry and machine gunners made their way towards a key position – the occupation of Emmitsburg Road – preliminary to the "grand charge" upon the High Water Mark, as fighters strafed the Union stronghold, and simulated artillery and mortar strikes detonated all over both sides of Emmitsburg Road.

Not only had the Union Marines posted the entanglements to obstruct the progress of their Southern counterparts, but also established fortified machine gun positions, called pill boxes. Chandler noted, "This or that squad had dragged a one-pounder (light field gun) with them and took a shot or two at a pill box, and then hurriedly moved on."[98]

As the battle approached a climactic conclusion, the Confederates seemed to run into some stiff opposition in and around the Codori house and farm buildings, which neither small-arms fire, machine-gun fire, nor light artillery fire could clear out, resulting in the troops who were attempting to capture that position calling for armor support to help.[99]

Four M1917 tanks rolled into action, two to the right of the Marine attack, and two on the left, and then "charged the enemy lines diagonally," *The Frederick Post* recorded. "The tanks appeared and went after a machine gun nest with machine gun fire and then contemptuously ignored the small arms fire and ironed out some barb wire entanglements," George M. Chandler wrote in 1922.[100]

The pair of tanks on the right of the Marine assault immediately made for the Codori house and outbuildings, *The Washington Post* noting that one of the pair of tanks was armed with a "one-pounder" gun, while the other was armed with machine guns, as were the two tanks on the left flank.[101]

"The tanks went sneeringly up to the Codori

> "Then came the tanks! Like lazy animals, already gorged with battle and bored with slaughter, they wobbled through the oatfields, converging on the Codori House, and at a few hundred yards began spitting flame and smoke from their one-pounders."
>
> *- The Baltimore Sun July 5, 1922*[103]

Three of the four M1917 tanks sent to Gettysburg for the Marine maneuvers appear in this photograph parked in the encampment.

house, around the barn, around to the back door, through the chicken yards, up the front porch, firing explosive shells (supposedly) through the windows," *The Sun* stated. "In a few moments they waddled away, and you could almost imagine them chuckling horribly, heading again toward the rear to sleep and snore until there was no more killing to do. The enemy in the Codori House was silenced forever."[102]

One of the tanks involved at the Codori house became a "causality" in the attack and was taken out of action by enemy fire.[103]

*Leatherneck Magazine,* in a July 1922 article, "Heard and seen at Gettysburg," wrote, "...the modern attack progressed smoothly and satisfactorily. Every man in the assaulting companies had eighty rounds of blanks to fire and with the machine guns, the tanks and the artillery all sounding off it was kind of nice to be deaf before you started."[104]

Once the Marines had seized both sides of the road and had driven off the Union defenders, producing a clear path to the High Water Mark, the charge was declared over, the officers calling it premised on the determination that, at this point, "the defenders in consequence would be so shaken in morale that their retreat would be inevitable and the position, Cemetery ridge, won (by the Marines portraying the Southern forces)," *The Washington Post* concluded.[105]

The day had not gone without a price. One Marine reportedly suffered non-life-threatening injuries, sustaining burns to the face and chest, when a smoke round went-off in his proximity of which he had not been aware.

*The Sun* reported that two Marines were injured during the attack. Private B. R. Davis, Fifth Regiment, was injured when setting-off a blank, black powder round to simulate a ground explosion for a camera crew filming the battle. The charge went off prematurely, and "Davis fell, badly burned on his face and hands....Davis will lose his eyesight temporarily." Corporal C.G. Clowers suffered similar injuries from another ground charge when it was ignited.[106]

## Marine honored

Aside from the raging mock battle, one of the highlights for the Marines themselves that occurred, following the reenactment of their version of a modern Pickett's Charge, was when one of the Marines was the awarded the Chevalier de la Legion of d'Honneur (Knight [Chevalier] of the Legion of Honor).

Captain Chandler wrote, in *Gettysburg, 1922,* that Major Maurice E. Shearer of the Marines Fifth Regiment was awarded the French Medal of Honor by Colonel G.A. L. Dumont, the French military attaché from the French Legation in Washington, D.C., around 2:30 p.m. before a "grand review" of the combined bands of the marines Fifth and Sixth regiments, and in the presence of Pennsylvania Governor Sproul. Colonel Dumont pinned the French Legion of Honor on Shearer's breast for his work in Belleau Woods, and "kissed him on both cheeks."[107]

Shearer was serving as a Marine observer at Gettysburg during the event when the presentation was made. He received the Chevalier de la Legion of d'Honneur insignia at Gettysburg for his role in leading the final assault that captured Belleau Wood from the Germans, thus ending the potential for a significant German advance on Paris.[108]

"At the conclusion of the review, the band marched off to 'The End of a Perfect Day,' and the pomp and circumstance of the Nation's birthday was completed," Chandler stated.[109]

Major Maurice E. Shearer

"Now that the smoke of battle has cleared and we are home again, our thoughts turn back to the people along our route to Gettysburg who were so kind and hospitable to us, and I can assure you that none were as hospitable as your good people of Frederick."

– Gen. Smedley Butler to Col. D. John Markey, president of the Frederick Chamber of Commerce,

July 14, 1922[1]

# CHAPTER 7

# BACK TO QUANTICO

With the Battle of Gettysburg re-fought and re-won, the Marines began breaking down Camp Harding on July 5. After a week on the Gettysburg battlefield, it was time to retrace their steps from the previous march north.

"Dawn cannot come to[o] soon for the leathernecks' battlefield encampment is a veritable sea of mud and the troops want to get away before the clouds empty more buckets of water upon them," *The Frederick Post* reported.[2]

A company of engineers left camp for Thurmont on July 5 to begin setting up the camp there.[3] Some planes returned to Quantico since they would only be needed for mail service and not maneuvers. The canvas White House was disassembled and shipped back to Quantico.[4]

For the remainder of the Marines, it was time to dry out from the rains of the previous week and begin packing. "Tents, bedding and other materials were laid out under the warm sun to dry and camp had its first fully clear day in a week," *The Sun* reported.[5] Trucks and tractors were dug from the mud

**Pages 148-149:** Camp Harding housed more than 5,000 Marines in a sprawling encampment that would now have to be packed up and prepared for the trip back to Quantico. The Marines had a reputation of leaving their immense campsites flawlessly clean and litter free.
**Page 150 Top:** Marines encamped at East Potomac Park preparatory to their march on Gettysburg. **Page 150 Bottom:** Marines take a break along the fence line they had constructed between Virginia Monument and their encampment. **Above:** General Smedley Butler (sitting in vehicle) confers with fellow officers at East

so that they would be able to leave the battlefield in the morning.

Although the Marines had felt somewhat snubbed by the town of Gettysburg during their time there, the town finally began realizing what they had when it was too late. "This town has found them a different body of troops than they thought, and now everyone seems to regret that the Marines were not given a more cordial reception on their arrival," *The (Frederick) News* reported.[6] Part of the softening attitude may have been that residents saw how anxious other towns were to have the Marines come visit them for maneuvers. Towns were already making requests to host the 1923 maneuvers.

"Scores of places throughout the country have asked for the camp next year, but it is the idea to have scenes of historical interest used regularly because of the peculiar adaptability for movements of troops and the lessons of patriotism they teach," *The Sun* reported.[7]

Manassas was mentioned as the favored location for maneuvers in 1923, but it actually would end up being held in New Market, Virginia. *The Sun* also noted that the publicity the Marines had received about the maneuvers had increased the Marine recruiting efforts around the country.[8]

### The return to Quantico

The return march began on Thursday morning, July 6 at 6 a.m. It was a retracing of the same route that the Marines had taken from Quantico to Gettysburg except for one difference. Instead of spend-

ing one night in Frederick and two nights in Rockville, the Marines spent two nights in Frederick and a single night in Rockville.

The Marines made a stop in Emmitsburg "to bid adieu to one of the most hospitable and picturesque little towns they have struck up an acquaintance with."[9] Although the Marines had been encamped on the southern end of Gettysburg on the battlefield, many of them had chosen to hike back to Emmitsburg to enjoy their free time rather than go into Gettysburg.[10]

The five living veterans of the Civil War, as well as hundreds of residents, were once again on hand to welcome the Marines back into Emmitsburg before they headed further south to their camp. As a sign of their fondness for the residents of the town, the Marines planned on sending a movie of the Marine's first visit in the town during the last week of June.[11]

As the Marines set up their camp on Hooker Lewis' farm just north of Thurmont around 2 p.m., Col. D. John Markey drove to Frederick to make arrangements for the Marine reception there.

## Frederick

The following afternoon, the Marines marched into Frederick as they had left it…singing. Camp was once again erected on the fairgrounds to the east of the city as had been done two weeks earlier.

Since the Marines had two nights to relax in Frederick, they made use of some of the facilities in the city. The YMCA pool may have been the most-popular site among the Marines. "At all hours the building was used by the soldiers who thoroughly enjoyed the facilities. The swimming pool and the showers were the greatest treat for the boys," reported *The (Gettysburg) Star and Sentinel.*[12] An estimated 1,000 Marines made use of the pool.[13]

On Saturday afternoon, Maryland Governor Albert Ritchie, Frederick Mayor Lloyd Culler, Adjutant General Milton A. Reckford, Major General John Lejeune, Acting Secretary of Navy Theodore Roosevelt, Jr., General Smedley Butler, Frederick City aldermen, and 50 of Butler's staff enjoyed a luncheon at Rose Hill Manor at a luncheon hosted by the Frederick Chamber of Commerce. At 2:30 p.m., the Marines began marching through Frederick in a grand parade that culminated with a review by Gov. Ritchie in front of the Frederick City Hall.[14]

During the late afternoon, the Marines enjoying the fairgrounds received a special visitor as President Harding and his party stopped by on their way back from Marion, Ohio. The Hardings' car stopped outside the camp and the president and his wife stood in the road as the Expeditionary Force Marine Corps Band serenaded them.

The band first played "The End of a Perfect Day," knowing it was Mrs. Harding's favorite song.

When they finished, the president asked, "Do you know 'The Long, Long Trail'?"

The band played the song in march time for the couple.

"That was splendid, boys, but you play it so fast. I'm so fond of that song that I like to have it last as long as possible when it is played," Mrs. Harding said.[15]

Gen. Butler started to support Mrs. Harding's position when the president said, "If you boys undertake to be directed by either the General or the 'boss' you'll get into trouble."

The band decided to play both songs again.[16]

That evening, the 135-member band (a combination of three bands) was again called on to perform. An estimated 5,000 people came into the city from Frederick County as well as other counties to hear the band perform at the Court House Park at 7:30 p.m. It was the largest open-air concert ever held in the city of Frederick.[17]

### The end of the road

The Marines left Frederick on Sunday morning, July 9, and marched to Ridgeville where they stayed the night. The next two nights they camped in Rockville and Bethesda, respectively.

At Bethesda, they once again camped on the Corby Estate. While the Marines spent part of the evening singing and watching champions from different companies box,[18] they also had to prepare for the next day. Gen. Butler was intent on making a good impression and presentation.

When the Marines had arrived in the capital on June 20, they had been fresh and clean. The march hadn't begun yet. They had only endured a ride on barges during the morning.

Now they were returning more than three weeks

President Warren G. Harding and members of the press at Camp Harding July 1, 1922.

# THE BLISTER

### G-BURG — July 5, 1922.

THE TRANSITION — HOW FAR OFF?

*The Blister* was an unofficial "almost daily" student publication at Gettysburg College. It made its first appearance on the bulletin board of Glatfelter Hall in 1921 offering opinions about campus life, cartoons, poems, and humorous anecdotes. It was single typewritten sheet that was published 1921-1927.

When the Marines approached Gettysburg, the Blister noted, "Girls! the marines are coming. But this is not war time; do not let them take your hearts by storm."[19]

However after they had left town, *The Blister* took a negative view of reenactments and war. "To the thoughtful, the demonstration brought another conviction—appeal to man's brutal nature and to the stormy youth, but they will not stand the test of reflection and common sense. Beneath the gorgeous of the sweep of power we can see little more than a tremendous waste of energy, time, money, life, and happiness, in sustaining a remnant of barbarism," *The Blister* noted.[20]

later, having slept in tents all of those nights. They had endured high heat and heavy rains. They had marched hundreds of miles and wanted to return to Quantico.

"On the instructions of Brig. Gen. Smedley D. Butler, commanding officer of the expeditionary force, kerosene was issued to the men of the artillery and truck train and all metal work was cleaned with oil so that on the arrival of the infantry it shone as though it had just been moved from the shop," *The Washington Post* reported.[21]

The next morning, the Marines marched on Washington. Secretary Roosevelt, on horseback, met them at Chevy Chase and rode with the Marines into the heart of Washington.[22] On their way back to East Potomac Park, the Marines marched past the White House once again. The president was otherwise engaged, but the first lady came out to greet the sea soldiers as they passed by the portico.[23]

The Marines camped that evening in East Potomac Park on Potomac River. The next morning they once again boarded barges, and Navy ships towed the men back to their base at Quantico ending their Gettysburg adventure.

"There is a wheat field nearby, and Marines seldom see a wheat field without seeing red. But they had come as...

"Rolling Kitchens had to be shunted off the road and hauled 300 yards across old plowed fields by hand. The same thing had to be done with the big water tanks the Marines are carrying with them. Every kitchen and tank required 20-manpower or more to handle it. Though they are here, between Bethesda and Rockville for one night, and a short night at that, every tent had to be put up, the radio aerials raised and the air searched for messages, mail brought in and sent out and "chow" cooked. So that one big 'gyrene' hauling on a ton of iron rolling kitchen spent a moment he should have used catching his breath to disclaim disgustedly:

"'The hoss Marines.'"

*- The Sun*, June 21, 1922[24]

**Page 154:** Marines pose for the photographer in their Gettysburg battlefield encampment, 1922. ***Below:*** Marines pose for the photographer while standing in their "chow line," 1922. **Pages 156-157:** Marines march in review past the White House on July 12 as First Lady Florence Harding looks on.

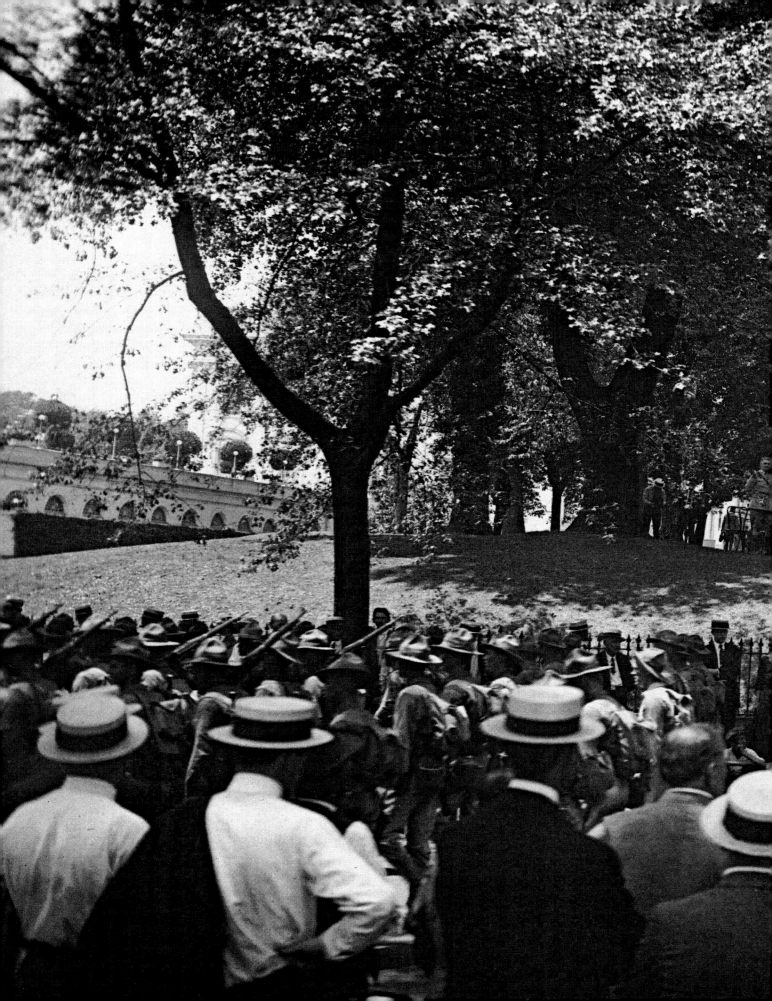

President Warren Harding relaxes during the 1922 Marine reenactment of Pickett's Charge at Gettysburg.

*This letter from a Marine who took part in the march was printed in The Gettysburg Times in 1972:*[25]

Your recent article on the 1922 visitation of 5,500 Marines coming to Gettysburg revives pleasant memories.

I was one of the 5,500 5th Regiment of Marines that arrived to re-enact the Battle as it was fought in the Civil War and the following day we re-enacted it according to the tactics of 1922 with a couple of Martin Bombers.

We marched as a group from Quantico, Va., with Smedley D. Butler ("Gimlet Eye") as commanding general. We camped overnight at various pre-arranged farmers' fields and camped in the general area of Lee's monument. The Field Hospital, of which I was a part, camped just below the monument.

The number of tourists, observing the activities were meager by today's standards.

Being loose of foot at the time and with idle thoughts that if in the fullness of time and life was fortunate that this was the ideal area, out of many, wherein I would finally hang up my knapsack. So, 21 years later while overseas I answered a Strout Ad and purchased the present place, sight unseen, and have camped here ever since getting out of the service after the war.

Thank you for the memories.

Yours truly,
Lieut. A. S. Bagley,
MSC USN Ret.

# NOT ALL WERE PLEASED

On a sour note, some of the troops participating in the Marine reenactment and military demonstrations held in Gettysburg during the fifty-ninth anniversary of the battle felt they could have had a better experience while in Gettysburg.

An article published in the July 7, 1922, *The Gettysburg Times* and in the July 8 issue of *The (Gettysburg) Star and Sentinel* noted that, "Gettysburg missed an opportunity to win the men of the United States Marines...according to a written statement made in behalf of the Marines by one of their number before the troops left Gettysburg (on July 6)" to begin their march back to Quantico.[26]

"Charges of snobbishness, over-charging, and petty trickery are made by a Marine spokesman, who declares the sea soldiers have no desire to return to Gettysburg," the article states.[27]

According to the newspaper, the spokesman wrote, "All along their line of march from Quantico to Emmitsburg, the Marines received tremendous ovations...There has been much adverse comment among the Marines in the manner in which they were received by Gettysburg residents upon their arrival...Their criticism came into being with what they called a cool attitude among the townsfolk towards them and swelled to prodigious proportions as cases of overcharging by merchants and instances of petty, but mean subterfuges by others were experienced by them."[28]

The spokesman also noted that the state shut-down the Marines' camp movie theater after it appeared that local theater operators complained that the troops showing movies in their encampment "interfered with local business," further noting that this was a first in the experience of the Marines who had shown their own camp movies in all of their previous encampments.[29]

"The Marines generally look upon Gettysburg as a town of money grabbers," the spokesman stated, adding that one Marine said, "They are welcoming us alright, but with itchy palms." He noted, "They are so used to being liked by people that running into an iceberg is not pleasant."[30]

"Some of our men have found unbounded hospitality in Gettysburg, but it was only on a small scale, and did not go the round," the Marine wrote.

"Bringing this out is bitter, but it is the truth, and unless a remedy is found, it shall live as long as

**"The Marines are desirous of showing Fredericktonians how much they appreciate the courtesy shown them on their visit recently to the historic city. They will be as spruce as elbow grease can make them. They would not go to greater effort even for President Harding..."**

*– The News*, July 6, 1922[32]

# THE MARINE CORPS BAND

The Marines have had a band for nearly as long as there have been Marines. "Fifes and drums were the only musical instruments used by our military in the Revolution. A group of ten or more of them was called a 'Band,' and those gallant Marines possessed as fine a 'Band' as any other military organization of the period," according to the *History of the Marine Band*.[33]

The band was officially recognized in 1798 when the positions of Drum Major and Fife Major were created and thirty-two drum and fifes were authorized when John Adams organized the Marines on July 11.[34]

Since that time until the 1922 march, the Marine Corps Band had sixteen leaders. The most famous of these was John Philip Sousa who led the band from Oct. 1, 1880 to July 30, 1892.[35]

When President Warren Harding reviewed the troops at the White House on June 20, a tradition was being repeated. The Marine Corps Band became the first troops reviewed by the president at the White House when Thomas Jefferson reviewed them on July 4, 1801.[36] Jefferson gave the band the title of "The President's Own."[37]

The Marine Corps Band is now a full band of wind, brass, percussion, pianos, and even vocalists. It also continues to generate positive public relations for the Marine Corps.

**Above:** Expeditionary Force Marine Band performs in front of the Canvas White House July 1, 1922. **Page 160:** Marines passing White House on their return to Quantico. **Pages 162-163:** First Lady Harding reviews the Marines July 12 as they pass the White House on their return to Quantico.

*The outdoor movie provided our evening entertainment.*

"WATER! WATER!"

*...and learned to live in the open.*

"Hey in there! Are yer blankets dry?"

Cartoons making fun about the amount of rain that fell during the 1922 maneuvers. These ran in *Leatherhead, the Story of Marine Corps Boot Camp* by Norval Eugene Packwood.

# ENDNOTES

**PREFACE**

1. R.S. T., "Gettysburg Pickett's Charge Dramatized in Marine Attack," *The (Baltimore) Sun*, July 2, 1922, 1.

**CHAPTER 1**

1. Tompkins, Raymond S., "Marines are marching on to Gettysburg," *The (Baltimore) Sun*, June 25, 1922, part 5, 4.
2. John Corrado, "What did the U.S. Marines do during the Civil War?" *The Straight Dope, Wesclark.com*, July 31, 2001 (http://wesclark.com/jw/usmc_in_cw.html) accessed January 9, 2015.
3. No author, "John J. Pershing quotes," *ThinkExist.com*, http://thinkexist.com/quotes/john_j._pershing/ (*accessed January 9, 2015*).
4. Authors interview with Gunnery Sergeant Thomas E. Williams (Ret.) Director of the United States Marine Corps Historical Company on December 12, 2014.
5. Williams interview.
6. United States Marine Corps, *United States Marine Barracks, Quantico* (Quantico, Va.: United States Marine Corps, 1930), 10.
7. Kenneth L. Smith-Christmas, "Marines at the Battle of the Wilderness," *Leatherneck*, September 2014, 19.
8. Unsigned article, "The Presidents and The Marines." *Marine Corps Gazette*, February 1933, 20-1.
9. Unsigned article, "Marines Begin Big Sham Battle," *(Gettysburg) Star & Sentinel*, October 1, 1921, 3.
10. Unsigned article, "Graysville Writes Army Life in Virginia," *The Sullivan (Ind.) Union*, October 26, 1921, 1.
11. Unsigned article, "Graysville Writes Army Life in Virginia," October 26, 1921.
12. Unsigned article, "Graysville Writes Army Life in Virginia," October 26, 1921.
13. Unsigned article, "Graysville Writes Army Life in Virginia," October 26, 1921.
14. Unsigned article, "Graysville Writes Army Life in Virginia," October 26, 1921.
15. Harry N. Price, "Harding Sees Battle," The Washington Post, October 2, 1921, 1.
16. H. K.. Reynolds, "Harding Tired After 'Battle'," *The Ogden (Utah) Standard-Examiner*, October 2, 1921, 13.
17. Harry N. Price, "Harding Sees Battle," October 2, 1921.
18. H. K. Reynolds, "Harding Tired After 'Battle'," October 2, 1921.
19. Unsigned article, *Boston Post*, "President Sees Army Camp Life," October 3, 1921, 8.
20. Unsigned article, "Graysville Writes Army Life in Virginia," October 26, 1921.

**CHAPTER 2**

1. Unsigned article, "5,000 Marines Camp at Maryland Line," *The (Baltimore) Sun*, June 20, 1922, 1.
2. Unsigned article, "Marines to 'Hike' to Gettysburg and Return," *The Leatherneck*, June 17, 1922. 1.
3. Unsigned article, "Will Make Plane Debut," *The Washington Post*, June 11, 1922, 19.
4. Unsigned article, "Marines Are On the March Here," *The Gettysburg Times*, June 20, 1922, 1.
5. Unsigned article, "President Saluted by 5,000 Marines," *The Washington Post*, June 20, 1922, 3.
6. Williams interview.
7. Unsigned article, "Marines Complete Hike Preparations," *The (Baltimore) Sun*, June 19, 1921, 3.
8. Tompkins, Raymond S., "Marines are marching on to Gettysburg," June 25, 1922.
9. Unsigned article, "5,000 Marines Camp at Maryland Line," June 20, 1922.
10. Unsigned article, "Marines Complete Hike Preparations," June 19, 1921.
11. William Tindall, *Standard History of the City of Washington From a Study of the Original Sources* (Knoxville, Tenn.: H.W. Crew & Co., 1914) 396.
12. U.S. Secretary of War Ad Interim, *Development of East Potomac Park* (Washington, D.C.: Government Printing Office, 1916) 10-11.
13. Unsigned article, "The Potomac Flats," *The Washington Post*, September 22, 1882, 1; U.S. Secretary of War Ad Interim, *Development of East Potomac Park*, 9.
14. Jon A. Peterson, *City Planning in the United States: 1840–1917* (Baltimore, Md.: The Johns Hopkins University Press, 2003) 78-91.
15. Tompkins, Raymond S., "Marines are marching on to Gettysburg," June 25, 1922.
16. Unsigned article, "Marines to 'Hike' to Gettysburg and Return," June 17, 1922.
17. Unsigned article, "5,000 Marines Camp at Maryland Line," June 20, 1922.
18. John DeFerrari, "Bread For The City: Shaw's Historic Bakeries," *Streets of Washington Stories and images of historic Washington*, http://www.streetsofwashington.com/2011/02/bread-for-city-shaws-historic-bakeries.html (accessed January 15, 2015).
19. John DeFerrari, "Bread For The City: Shaw's Historic Bakeries," *Streets of Washington Stories and images of historic Washington*.
20. John DeFerrari, "Bread For The City: Shaw's Historic Bakeries," *Streets of Washington Stories and images of historic Washington*.
21. "The Mansion at Strathmore History & Architecture," *Mansion at Strathmore*, http://www.strathmore.org/media/pdf/MansionHistory_final.pdf (accessed January 15, 2015).
22. Capt. John H. Craige, "The Marines at Gettysburg," *Marine Corps Gazette*, September 1922, 250.

23. Unsigned article, "President Saluted by 5,000 Marines," June 20, 1922.

24. Unsigned article, "Marine Army Sees Movies Of Itself on Eve of 'War'," *The Washington Post*, June 21, 1921, 7.

25. Tompkins, Raymond S., "Marines are marching on to Gettysburg," June 25, 1922.

26. Unsigned article, "5,000 Marines Camp at Maryland Line," June 20, 1922.

27. Unsigned article, "Marine Army Sees Movies Of Itself on Eve of 'War'," June 21, 1922.

28. Capt. John H. Craige, "The Marines at Gettysburg," September 1922.

29. Unsigned article, "Marines Rest In The Hills On Their Way To Gettysburg," *The (Baltimore) Sun*, June 23, 1922, 2; Unsigned article, "Graysville Writes Army Life in Virginia," October 26, 1921.

30. Unsigned article, "Rockville, in Gala Attire, Greets Army of Marines," *The Washington Post*, June 22, 1922, 8.

31. Unsigned article, "Marylanders 'Snipe' Marines With Fruit And Cool Drinks," *The (Baltimore) Sun*, June 22, 1922, 2.

32. Tom Alciere, "RE: Alfred C. Tolson, Maryland," *Ancestry.com*, http://boards.ancestry.com/thread.aspx?mv=flat&m=23&p=surnames.tolson (accessed January 21, 2015).

33. Unsigned article, "Marines Rest In The Hills On Their Way To Gettysburg," June 23, 1922.

34. Unsigned article, "Marines Pitch Tents For Night In Daisy Fields Of Maryland," *The (Baltimore) Sun*, June 21, 1922, 2.

35. Unsigned article, "Marines Pitch Tents For Night In Daisy Fields Of Maryland," June 21, 1922.

36. Ben Franklin, "Chevrolet House in the Suburb Primeval," Town of Garrett Park, http://www.garrettpark-md.gov/c/289/architecture (accessed January 14, 2015).

37. Ben Franklin, "Chevrolet House in the Suburb Primeval," *Town of Garrett Park*.

38. Unsigned article, "5,000 Marines Camp at Maryland Line," June 20, 1922.

39. Unsigned article, "Marine Army Sees Movies Of Itself on Eve of 'War'," June 21, 1922.

40. Unsigned article, "Mimic War Serious Play, Marines Find on the March," *The Washington Post*, July 3, 1922, 3.

41. Unsigned article, "Mimic War Serious Play, Marines Find on the March," July 3, 1922.

42. Unsigned article, "On Their Way to Gettysburg," Montgomery County Sentinel, June 23, 1922, 3.

43. Unsigned article, "Marylanders 'Snipe' Marines With Fruit And Cool Drinks," June 22, 1922.

44. Unsigned article, "Marylanders 'Snipe' Marines With Fruit And Cool Drinks," June 22, 1922.

45. Unsigned article, "Marylanders 'Snipe' Marines With Fruit And Cool Drinks," June 22, 1922.

46. Unsigned article, "Rockville, in Gala Attire, Greets Army of Marines," June 22, 1922.

47. Unsigned article, "Marines Stage Big Battle, Then Lose at Baseball," *The Washington Post*, June 23, 1922, 1.

48. Unsigned article, "Marines Stage Big Battle, Then Lose at Baseball," June 23, 1922.

49. Unsigned article, "Marines Complete Hike Preparations," June 19, 1921.

50. Tompkins, Raymond S., "Marines are marching on to Gettysburg," June 25, 1922.

51. Unsigned article, "Marines Pitch Tents For Night In Daisy Fields Of Maryland," June 21, 1922.

52. Unsigned article, "Marines Pitch Tents For Night In Daisy Fields Of Maryland," June 21, 1922.

53. R. S. T., "Marines to Begin Rehearsals of Pickett's Charge Today," The (Baltimore Sun), June 28, 1922, 1.

54. Unsigned article, "Marines Complete Hike Preparations," June 19, 1921.

55. Unsigned article, "Marylanders 'Snipe' Marines With Fruit And Cool Drinks," June 22, 1922.

56. Unsigned article, "Marines Rest In The Hills On Their Way To Gettysburg," June 23, 1922.

57. Unsigned article, "Marines Rest In The Hills On Their Way To Gettysburg," June 23, 1922.

58. Unsigned article, "Marines Rest In The Hills On Their Way To Gettysburg," June 23, 1922.

59. Unsigned article, "5,000 Marines Camp At Ridgeville; Corps Reach Frederick At Noon Today," *The Frederick Post*, June 24, 1922, 1.

60. Unsigned article, "Marine Army Sees Movies Of Itself on Eve of 'War'," June 21, 1922.

61. Unsigned article, "On Their Way to Gettysburg," June 23, 1922.

62. Unsigned article, "Marines Pitch Tents For Night In Daisy Fields Of Maryland," June 21, 1922.

63. Unsigned article, "Frederick Welcomes 5,000 Marines Arriving At Noon For Day's Stay While Enroute To Gettysburg," *The (Frederick) News*, June 24, 1922, 1.

64. Unsigned article, "Frederick Welcomes 5,000 Marines Arriving At Noon For Day's Stay While Enroute To Gettysburg," June 24, 1922.

65. Unsigned article, "Road-Weary Marines Find Frederick's Gates Wide Open," *The (Baltimore) Sun*, June 25, 1922, 4.

66. Unsigned article, "Road-Weary Marines Find Frederick's Gates Wide Open," June 25, 1922.

67. Unsigned article, "Frederick Welcomes 5,000 Marines Arriving At Noon For Day's Stay While Enroute To Gettysburg," June 24, 1922.

68. Unsigned article, "Frederick Welcomes 5,000 Marines Arriving At Noon For Day's Stay While Enroute To Gettysburg," June 24, 1922.

69. Unsigned article, "Marines Complete Hike Reaching Camp Gettysburg Today," *The (Frederick) News*, June 26, 1922, 5.

70. Mark Ziegler, "History – 1922, Class D, Blue Ridge League - Chapter 7, 1922 – Martinsburg Sluggers Rawlings and Wilson's Record Breaking Seasons Leave The Rest of the League 'Blue' with Envy," *Class D Blue Ridge League*, http://www.blueridgeleague.org/1922.asp (accessed January 19, 2015).

71. Unsigned article, "Blue Ridge League," *The (Frederick) News*, June 26, 1922, 3.

72. Unsigned article, "Modern 'Barbara Frietchies' Greet Marines In Frederick," *The (Baltimore) Sun*, June 26, 1922, 2.

73. Unsigned article, "Marines At Camp Harding On Historic Field Today," *The Washington Post*, June 26, 1922, 2.

74. Unsigned article, "5,000 Marines Camp At Ridgeville; Corps Reach Frederick At Noon Today," June 24, 1922.

75. Unsigned article, "Marines on Way to Town," *Gettysburg Compiler*, June 24, 1922, 1.

76. Unsigned article, "Modern 'Barbara Frietchies' Greet Marines In Frederick," June 26, 1922.

77. Unsigned article, "Modern 'Barbara Frietchies' Greet Marines In Frederick," June 26, 1922.

78. Unsigned article, "Modern 'Barbara Frietchies' Greet Marines In Frederick," June 26, 1922.

79. Unsigned article, "Modern 'Barbara Frietchies' Greet Marines In Frederick," June 26, 1922.

80. Unsigned article, "Modern 'Barbara Frietchies' Greet Marines In Frederick," June 26, 1922.

81. Unsigned article, "Marines Camp Here," *Catoctin Clarion*, June 29, 1922, 3.

82. Tompkins, Raymond S., "Marines are marching on to Gettysburg," June 25, 1922.

83. Unsigned article, "Marylanders 'Snipe' Marines With Fruit And Cool Drinks," June 22, 1922.

84. Unsigned article, "Marines Camp Here," June 29, 1922.

85. Unsigned article, "On Their Way to Gettysburg," June 23, 1922.

86. Unsigned article, "Marines Camp Here," June 29, 1922.

87. Unsigned article, "Road-Weary Marines Find Frederick's Gates Wide Open," June 25, 1922.

88. Unsigned article, "Mimic War Serious Play, Marines Find On The March," July 3, 1922.

89. Unsigned article, "Modern 'Barbara Frietchies' Greet Marines In Frederick," June 26, 1922.

90. Unsigned article, "Modern 'Barbara Frietchies' Greet Marines In Frederick," June 26, 1922.

91. Unsigned article, "Modern 'Barbara Frietchies' Greet Marines In Frederick," June 26, 1922.

92. Unsigned article, "Mimic War Serious Play, Marines Find On The March," July 3, 1922.

93. Unsigned article, "Marine Camp Is Being Laid out," *Gettysburg Times*, June 20, 1922, 1.

94. Unsigned article, "Mimic War Serious Play, Marines Find On The March," July 3, 1922.

95. Unsigned article, "Marines Complete Hike Reaching Camp Gettysburg Today," June 26, 1922 1.

96. Tompkins, Raymond S., "Marines are marching on to Gettysburg," June 25, 1922; Unsigned article, "Veterans of '61 See Marine Army Invade Scarred Gettysburg Field," The Washington Post, June 27, 1922, 2.

97. Unsigned article, "Marines Rest In The Hills On Their Way To Gettysburg," June 23, 1922; Unsigned article, "Graysville Writes Army Life in Virginia," October 26, 1921.

98. Tompkins, Raymond S., "Marines are marching on to Gettysburg," June 25, 1922.

99. Unsigned article, "Marine Hikers Test Hero's War Device," *The Washington Post*, June 25, 1922, 12.

100. Unsigned article, "Marine Hikers Test Hero's War Device," June 25, 1922.

101. Unsigned article, "Marines Rest In The Hills On Their Way To Gettysburg," June 23, 1922.

102. Unsigned article, "Marines Rest In The Hills On Their Way To Gettysburg," June 23, 1922.

**CHAPTER 3**

1. R. S. T., "Marines to Begin Rehearsals of Pickett's Charge Today," June 28, 1922.

2. Unsigned article, "Canvas City to be Raised Here," *The Gettysburg Times*, June 16, 1922, 4.

3. Unsigned article, "Camp is being Shaken Down," The *Gettysburg Times*, June 27, 1922, 2.

4. Unsigned article, "Pickett's Charge," *Historynet.com*, http://www.historynet.com/picketts-charge-gettysburg (accessed January 1, 2015).

5. Unsigned article. "Pickett's Charge," *Historynet.com.*

6. Unsigned article, "Military History Online - Battle of Gettysburg," Militaryhistoryonline.com. (accessed January 1, 2015).

7. Pam Newhouse and Renae Hardoby, *The Codori Family and Farm: In the Path of Battle* (Gettysburg, PA: Friends of the National Parks at Gettysburg, 1999), 42.

8. Unsigned article, "Pays Visit by Aeroplane," *The Gettysburg Times*, June 23, 1922, 1.

9. Unsigned article, "Pays Visit by Aeroplane," June 23, 1922.

10. Unsigned article, "Pays Visit by Aeroplane," June 23, 1922.

11. J. R. McCarl, "Continuous Air Voyages for Travel-Expense Purposes," Decisions of the Comptroller General of the United States 2.June 1, 1922-July 30, 1923 (1923), 287-89.

12. Unsigned article, "J. Parker Van Zandt," *Davis-Monthan Airfield Register*, Dmairfield.org, February 11, 2006, http://dmairfield.org/register_listings.php (accessed January 29, 2015).

13. M. Birtwistle, "The Hospital Corps with the Marine Expeditionary Force in the 1922 Spring Exercises," *The Supplement to the United States Naval Medical Bulletin 1922*, ser. 6.4 (1923), 55. (Published as a supplement to *The Hospital Corps Quarterly & Supplement to the United States Naval Medical Bulletin* of January 1921.)

14. M. Birtwistle, "The Hospital Corps with the Marine Expeditionary Force in the 1922 Spring Exercises," 55.

15. M. Birtwistle, "The Hospital Corps with the Marine Expeditionary Force in the 1922 Spring Exercises," 55.

16. M. Birtwistle, "The Hospital Corps with the Marine Expeditionary Force in the 1922 Spring Exercises," 55.

17. M. Birtwistle, "The Hospital Corps with the Marine Expeditionary Force in the 1922 Spring Exercises," 55.

18. M. Birtwistle, "The Hospital Corps with the Marine Expeditionary Force in the 1922 Spring Exercises," 55.

19. M. Birtwistle, "The Hospital Corps with the Marine Expeditionary Force in the 1922 Spring Exercises," 55.

20. M. Birtwistle, "The Hospital Corps with the Marine Expeditionary Force in the 1922 Spring Exercises," 55.

21. Unsigned article, "Hospital Unit Arrives at Camp," *The Gettysburg Times*, June 30, 1922, 3.

22. Unsigned article, "Hospital Unit Arrives at Camp," June 30, 1922.

23. Unsigned article, "Hospital Unit Arrives at Camp," June 30, 1922.

24. Unsigned article, "Hospital Unit Arrives at Camp," June 30, 1922.

25. Unsigned article, "Air Mail Service," *The Gettysburg Times*, June 27, 1922, 1.

26. Unsigned article, "Air Mail Service," June 27, 1922.

27. Unsigned article, "Air Mail Service," June 27, 1922.

28. Unsigned article, "Canvas City to be Raised Here," June 16, 1922.

29. Unsigned article, "Canvas City to be Raised Here," June 16, 1922.

30. Unsigned article, "Canvas City to be Raised Here," June 16, 1922.

31. Unsigned article, "Canvas City to be Raised Here," June 16, 1922.

32. Unsigned article, "Harding Party Coming Saturday," *The Gettysburg Times*, July 27, 1922, 1; Unsigned article, "Harding Made Brief Visit Here," *The Gettysburg Times*, July 3, 1922, 1.

33. Authors telephone interview with Gunnery Sergeant Thomas E. Williams (Ret.) Director of the United States Marine Corps Historical Company on January 29, 2015.

34. Unsigned article, "Canvas City to be Raised Here," June 16, 1922.

35. R. S. T., "Harding to View Marines in New Pickett's Charge," *The (Baltimore) Sun*, June 30, 1922, 9.

36. Unsigned article, "Marine Camp Is Being Laid out," June 20, 1922.
37. Unsigned article, "Marine Camp Is Being Laid out," June 20, 1922.
38. Unsigned article, "Bombing Planes are Brought Here," *The Gettysburg Times,* June 24, 1922, 1; Unsigned article, "Harding to be Here July 3 and 4," *The Gettysburg Times,* June 23, 1922, 1.
39. Unsigned article, "Marine Camp Is Being Laid out," June 20, 1922; Unsigned article, "Camp is being Shaken Down," June 27, 1922.
40. R. S. T., "Marines to Begin Rehearsals of Pickett's Charge Today," June 28, 1922.
41. Unsigned article, "Accidents Mar Camp Opening," *The Gettysburg Times,* June 27, 1922, 3.
42. R. S. T., "Harding to View Marines in New Pickett's Charge," June 30, 1922.
43. Unsigned article, "Marine Camp Is Being Laid out," June 20, 1922; R. S. T., "Marines to Begin Rehearsals of Pickett's Charge Today," June 28, 1922.
44. Unsigned article, "Marine Camp Is Being Laid out," June 20, 1922.
45. Unsigned article, "Camp is being Shaken Down," June 27, 1922.
46. Unsigned article, "Camp is being Shaken Down," June 27, 1922.
47. Unsigned article, "Harding Will Review Marines," *The Gettysburg Times,* June 19, 1922, 1.
48. R. S. T., "Two Marine Aviators Killed on Gettysburg Battlefield," *The (Baltimore) Sun,* June 27, 1922, 1.
49. Unsigned article, "Have Equipment for Division," *The Gettysburg Times,* June 26, 1922, 1.
50. R. S. T., "Two Marine Aviators Killed on Gettysburg Battlefield," June 27, 1922.
51. Raymond S. Tompkins, "Marines on Edge at Gettysburg to Reenact Great Battle Today," *The (Baltimore) Sun,* July 1, 1922, 7.
52. R. S. T., "Marines to Begin Rehearsals of Pickett's Charge Today," June 28, 1922.
53. Unsigned article, "White House is Being Erected," *The Gettysburg Times,* June 28, 1922, 3; R. S. T., "Marines to Begin Rehearsals of Pickett's Charge Today," June 28, 1922.
54. Unsigned article, "White House is Being Erected," June 28, 1922.
55. Unsigned article, "Bombing Planes are Brought Here," June 24, 1922; Unsigned article, "Harding Party Coming Saturday," July 27, 1922.
56. Unsigned article, "White House is Being Erected," June 28, 1922.
57. Unsigned article., "Canvas City to be Raised Here," June 16, 1922; Unsigned article, "Harding Made Brief Visit Here," July 3, 1922.
58. Unsigned article, "White House is Being Erected," June 28, 1922.
59. Unsigned article, "Dress Rehearsal for the Charge," *The Gettysburg Times,* June 30, 1922, 3.
60. R. S. T., "Marines to Begin Rehearsals of Pickett's Charge Today," June 28, 1922.
61. Unsigned article, "White House is Being Erected," June 28, 1922.
62. Unsigned article, "White House is Being Erected," June 28, 1922.
63. Unsigned article, "White House is Being Erected," June 28, 1922.
64. Unsigned article, "Dress Rehearsal for the Charge," June 30, 1922.
65. Unsigned article, "Camp made ready for president," *The Gettysburg Times,* June 29, 1922, 1.
66. Raymond S. Tompkins, "Marines Plan to Reenact Famous Battle Every Year," *The (Baltimore) Sun*, July 3, 1922, 3.
67. Clayton Barrow, Jr., "Looking for John A. Lejeune," *Marine Corps Gazette* [Quantico], April 1990.
68. Unsigned article, "White House is Being Erected," June 28, 1922.
69. R. S. T., "Marines to Begin Rehearsals of Pickett's Charge Today," June 28, 1922.
70. Unsigned article, "Encampment to be Advertised," *The Gettysburg Times,* June 17, 1922, 1; Unsigned article, "Harding Will Review Marines," June 19, 1922.
71. Unsigned article, "Encampment to be Advertised," June 17, 1922.
72. Unsigned article, "Encampment to be Advertised," June 17, 1922.
73. Unsigned article, "Marines on Way to Town," June 24, 1922.
74. Unsigned article, "Encampment to be Advertised," June 17, 1922.
75. Unsigned article, "Encampment to be Advertised," June 17, 1922.
76. Unsigned article, "One Excursion Listed," *The Gettysburg Times,* June 21, 1922, 1.
77. Unsigned article, "Pathe Weekly Men Here," *The Gettysburg Times,* June 28, 1922, 2.
78. Unsigned article, "Pathe Weekly Men Here," June 28, 1922.
79. R. S. T., "Cemetery Hill Capitulates to Marine Attack," *The (Baltimore) Sun*, July 5, 1922, 1.
80. R. S. T., "Cemetery Hill Capitulates to Marine Attack," July 5, 1922; Unsigned article, "Marines Thrill 125,000 with Modern Maneuvers," *The Washington Post*, July 5, 1922, 5.
81. R. S. T., "Harding to View Marines in New Pickett's Charge," June 30, 1922.
82. Capt. John H. Craige, "The Marines at Gettysburg," September 7, 1922.

**CHAPTER 4**

1. Robert Debs Heinl, Jr., Dictionary of Military and Naval Quotations (Annapolis, MD: United States Naval Institute, 1966), 6.
2. Unsigned article, "The Aircraft Squadrons," *Marine Barracks, Quantico, Virginia. 1930* ed. (Quantico: Marine Barracks, 1930), 29.
3. Unsigned article, "Birth of the U.S. Marine Corps," History.com, A&E Television Networks, http://www.history.com/this-day-in-history/birth-of-the-us-marine-corps (accessed January 29. 2015).
4. Edward C. Johnson, "Marine Aviation in World War I, 1917-1918," *Marine Corps Aviation: The Early Years 1912-1940.* (Washington, D.C.: History and Museums Division, Headquarters, U.S. Marine Corps, 1977), 11.
5. Edward C. Johnson, "Marine Aviation in World War I, 1917-1918," *Marine Corps Aviation: The Early Years 1912-1940,* 9-59.
6. Edward C. Johnson, "Marine Aviation in World War I, 1917-1918," *Marine Corps Aviation: The Early Years 1912-1940*, 11.
7. Unsigned article, "De Havilland DH4 Fact Sheet," National Museum of the U.S. Air Force, http://www.nationalmuseum.af.mil/factsheets/factsheet.asp?id=324 (accessed January 4, 2015).

8. Unsigned article, "De Havilland DH4 Fact Sheet," National Museum of the U.S. Air Force, http://www.nationalmuseum.af.mil/factsheets/factsheet.asp?id=324 (accessed January 4, 2015); E. R. Johnson, "Heavier-than-air Development," *United States Naval Aviation, 1919-1941: Aircraft, Airships and Ships Between the Wars* (Jefferson, NC: McFarland, 2011), 11.

9. E. R. Johnson, "Heavier-than-air Development," *United States Naval Aviation, 1919-1941: Aircraft, Airships and Ships Between the Wars*, 11.

10. Unsigned Article, "Products: VE-7," Vought Heritage, http://www.vought.org/products/html/ve-7.html (accessed January 5, 2015).

11. E. R. Johnson, "Heavier-than-air Development," *United States Naval Aviation, 1919-1941: Aircraft, Airships and Ships Between the Wars*, 11.

12. Unsigned article, "Air Mail Service," June 27, 1922.

13. Unsigned article, "The Aircraft Squadrons." United States Marine Corps, 29; Unsigned article, "Marine Aviators Commended for Work During Maneuvers," *Leatherneck Magazine*, July 5 (1922), 1.

14. Mark Mortensen, *George W. Hamilton, USMC: America's Greatest World War 1 Hero* (Jefferson, NC: McFarland, 2011), 236; Unsigned article, "Marine Aviators Commended for Work During Maneuvers," 1.

15. Unsigned article, "Marines Awaken New Life on Famed Gettysburg Field," *The Washington Post*, June 28, 1922, 2.

16. Unsigned article, "Marine Corps Fliers at Gettysburg," *United States Air Services*, August 7 (1922), 28.

17. Unsigned article, "Marine Corps Fliers at Gettysburg," 28.

18. Unsigned article, "Marine Corps Fliers at Gettysburg," 28.

19. Unsigned article, "Accidents Mar Camp Opening," June 27, 1922.

20. Unsigned article, "Accidents Mar Camp Opening," June 27, 1922.

21. Unsigned article, "Accidents Mar Camp Opening," June 27, 1922; Unsigned article, "Wrecked Planes Removed to Camp," *The Gettysburg Times*, June 27, 1922, 1.

22. Unsigned article, "Accidents Mar Camp Opening," June 27, 1922.

23. Unsigned article, "Captain Hamilton and Sergeant Martin Killed When Plane Fell," *The (Gettysburg) Star and Sentinal*, July 1, 1922, 1; R. S. T., "Marine Aviators Crash to Death on Battlefield of Gettysburg," June 27, 1922.

24. R. S. T., "Marine Aviators Crash to Death on Battlefield of Gettysburg," The (Baltimore), June 27, 1922, 1.

25. Unsigned article, "Captain Hamilton and Sergeant Martin Killed When Plane Fell," July 1, 1922.

26. R. S. T., "Marine Aviators Crash to Death on Battlefield of Gettysburg," June 27, 1922.

27. Unsigned article, "Captain Hamilton and Sergeant Martin Killed When Plane Fell," July 1, 1922.

28. Unsigned article, "Marine Aviation," *Aviation*, July 17 (1922), 77.

29. Unsigned article, "Marine Aviation," 77.

30. Unsigned article, "Death of Captain Hamilton and Sergeant Martin Saddens Troops," *Leatherneck Magazine*, July 1922.

31. Unsigned article, "Captain Hamilton and Sergeant Martin Killed When Plane Fell," July 1, 1922.

32. R. S. T., "Marine Aviators Crash to Death on Battlefield of Gettysburg," June 27, 1922.

33. Unsigned article, "Captain Hamilton and Sergeant Martin Killed When Plane Fell," July 1, 1922.

34. R. S. T., "Marine Aviators Crash to Death on Battlefield of Gettysburg," June 27, 1922.

35. R. S. T., "Marine Aviators Crash to Death on Battlefield of Gettysburg," June 27, 1922.

36. R. S. T., "Marine Aviators Crash to Death on Battlefield of Gettysburg," June 27, 1922.

37. R. S. T., "Marine Aviators Crash to Death on Battlefield of Gettysburg," June 27, 1922.

38. Unsigned article, "Wrecked Planes Removed to Camp," June 27, 1922.

39. Unsigned article, "Wrecked Planes Removed to Camp," June 27, 1922.; Unsigned article, "Metal Sold for Junk," *The Gettysburg Times*, June 27, 1922, 1.

40. Unsigned article, "Metal Sold for Junk," June 27, 1922

41. Unsigned article, "Metal Sold for Junk," June 27, 1922; Unsigned article, "Wrecked Planes Removed to Camp," June 27, 1922.

42. Unsigned article, "Death of Captain Hamilton and Sergeant Martin Saddens Troops," July 1922.

43. Unsigned article, "Attend Funeral of Dead Aviator," *The Gettysburg Times*, June 29, 1922, 1.

44. Unsigned article, "5,000 See Hero Die," *The Washington Post*, June 27, 1922, 1.

45. Unsigned article, "Attend Funeral of Dead Aviator," June 29, 1922.

46. Unsigned article, "Obituary: Mrs. Ida Margaret Hamilton," *Army and Navy Register*, January 5 LXIII 1955 (1918), 535.

47. Edward C. Johnson, "Marine Aviation in World War I, 1917-1918," *Marine Corps Aviation: The Early Years 1912-1940*, 77.

48. Unsigned article, "Marine Aviation," 77.

49. Unsigned article, "Biographies," *Who's Who in the Nation's Capital 1921-1922, (*Washington, D.C.: Consolidated, 1921), 164.

50. Unsigned article, "Marine Aviation," 77.

51. Unsigned article, "Notes from the Air," *U.S. Air Service*, August VII.7 (1922), 37.

52. Kemper F. Cowing, "The Quality of a Hero," *Dear Folks at Home - - -*, (Boston & New York: Houghton Mifflin, 1919), 129.

53. Unsigned article, "Military Rites for Dead Aviator," June 28, 1922.

54. Unsigned article, "Biographies," 164.

55. Unsigned article, "Marine Aviation," 77.

56. Unsigned article, "Military Rites for Dead Aviator," *The Gettysburg Times*, June 28, 1922, 1.

57. Unsigned article, "Military Rites for Dead Aviator," June 28, 1922.

58. Unsigned article, "Marines Rehearse Pickett's Famed Gettysburg Charge," *The New York Times*, June 29, 1922, 1; Unsigned article, "Military Rites for Dead Aviator," June 28, 1922.

59. Unsigned article, "Military Rites for Dead Aviator," June 28, 1922.

## CHAPTER 5

1. Unsigned article, "Marines Charge as Pickett Did on Gettysburg's Field," *The Washington Post*, June 30, 1922, 2.

2. Unsigned article, "Marines Arrive in Camp Here," *The Gettysburg Times*, June 26, 1922, 1.

3. Unsigned article, "Marines Arrive in Camp Here," June 26, 1922.

4. Unsigned article, "Marines Arrive in Camp Here," June 26, 1922.

5. R. S. T., "Two Marine Aviators Killed on Gettysburg Battlefield," June 27, 1922.
6. Unsigned article. "Camp Is Being Shaken Down," June 27, 1922.
7. Unsigned article, "Marines Arrive in Camp Here," June 26, 1922.
8. Unsigned article, "Marines View Battlefield," *The Gettysburg Times,* June 28, 1922, 1; Unsigned article, "Maneuvers a Feature of the Day," *The Gettysburg Times* June 28, 1922: 3.
9. R. S. T., "Two Marine Aviators Killed on Gettysburg Battlefield," June 27, 1922.
10. Unsigned article. "Camp Is Being Shaken Down," June 27, 1922.
11. R. S. T., "Marines Are Told the Story of Battle," *The (Baltimore) Sun,* June 29, 1922, 2.
12. R. S. T., "Marines Are Told the Story of Battle," June 29, 1922.
13. Unsigned article, "Marines Charge as Pickett Did on Gettysburg's Field," June 30, 1922.
14. Raymond S. Tompkins, "Gettysburg, As Leathernecks See It," *The (Baltimore) Sun,* July 2, 1922, MS12.
15. Unsigned article, "Canvas City to be Raised Here," June 16, 1922.
16. Unsigned article, "Harding Will Review Marines," June 19, 1922; Unsigned article, "Canvas City to be Raised Here," June 16, 1922.
17. Unsigned article, "Harding Will Review Marines," June 19, 1922; M. Birtwistle, "The Hospital Corps with the Marine Expeditionary Force in the 1922 Spring Exercises," 55.
18. R. S. T., "Marines to Begin Rehearsals of Pickett's Charge Today," June 28, 1922.
19. R. S. T., "Marines to Begin Rehearsals of Pickett's Charge Today," June 28, 1922.
20. R. S. T., "Marines to Begin Rehearsals of Pickett's Charge Today," June 28, 1922.
21. R. S. T., "Marines to Begin Rehearsals of Pickett's Charge Today," June 28, 1922.
22. R. S. T., "Marines Are Told the Story of Battle," June 29, 1922.
23. John D. Wright, *The Language of the Civil War* (Westport, CT: Oryx, 2001) 48.
24. R. S. T., "Marines Are Told the Story of Battle," June 29, 1922.
25. Unsigned article, "Marines Rehearse Pickett's Famed Gettysburg Charge," June 29, 1922.
26. R. S. T., "Marines Are Told the Story of Battle," June 29, 1922; United States. National Park Service, "The Gettysburg Cyclorama," *National Parks Service,* U.S. Department of the Interior, http://www.nps.gov/gett/learn/historyculture/gettysburg-cyclorama.htm (accessed January 15, 2015).
27. Unsigned article, "Marines Awaken New Life on Famed Gettysburg Field," June 28, 1922.
28. Unsigned article, "Attack Made on Seminary Ridge," *Star and Sentinel* (Gettysburg), July 1, 1922, 3.
29. Unsigned article, "Maneuvers a Feature of the Day," June 28, 1922.
30. Unsigned article, "Maneuvers a Feature of the Day," June 28, 1922.
31. Unsigned article, "Marines Rehearse Pickett's Famed Gettysburg Charge," June 29, 1922.
32. Unsigned article, "Marines View Battlefield," June 28, 1922.
33. Unsigned article, "Marines View Battlefield," June 28, 1922; Unsigned article, "Marines Rehearse Pickett's Famed Gettysburg Charge," June 29, 1922.
34. R. S. T., "Marines Are Told the Story of Battle," June 29, 1922.
35. R. S. T., "Marines Are Told the Story of Battle," June 29, 1922.
36. Unsigned article, "Attaches Arrive at Camp Harding," *The Gettysburg Times,* June 28, 1922, 1; Unsigned article, "Harding and Pershing View Re-enactment of Pickett's Charge," *The Gettysburg Times,* July 3, 1922, 1.
37. Unsigned article, "Attaches Arrive at Camp Harding," June 28, 1922; Unsigned article, "Harding and Pershing View Re-enactment of Pickett's Charge," July 3, 1922; Unsigned article, "Marine Officer Was Decorated," *The Star and Sentinel* (Gettysburg), July 8, 1922, 5; Unsigned article, "Harding Made Brief Visit Here," July 3, 1922.
38. Donald Langmead, "The Rise of the Rising Sun," *Icons of American Architecture: From the Alamo to the World Trade Center* (Westport, CT: Greenwood, 2009), 456.
39. Unsigned article, "The Tokyo War Crimes Trial," *Arthur J. Morris Law Library,* University of Virginia School of Law, http://lib.law.virginia.edu/imtfe (accessed January 31, 2015).
40. R. S. T., "Marines Are Told the Story of Battle," June 29, 1922.
41. Unsigned article, "Marines Rehearse Pickett's Famed Gettysburg Charge," June 29, 1922.
42. Unsigned article, "Large Attack Is Launched," *The Gettysburg Times,* June 30, 1922, 1.
43. Unsigned article, "Large Attack Is Launched," June 30, 1922.
44. Unsigned article, "Large Attack Is Launched," June 30, 1922.
45. Unsigned article, "Large Attack Is Launched," June 30, 1922.
46. Unsigned article, "United States Marines," *Gettysburg Compiler,* July 8, 1922, 1.
47. Unsigned article, "Large Attack Is Launched," June 30, 1922.
48. R. S. T., "Marines Are Told the Story of Battle," June 29, 1922.
49. Unsigned article, "Attack Made on Seminary Ridge," July 1, 1922.
50. Unsigned article, "Attack Made on Seminary Ridge," July 1, 1922.
51. Frank A. Mallen, "Whitehouse is being Built for Harding Guests," *The Frederick Post,* June 28, 1922, 1.
52. Unsigned article, "Marines View Battlefield," June 28, 1922.
53. Unsigned article, "Large Attack Is Launched," June 30, 1922.
54. Unsigned article, "Large Attack Is Launched," June 30, 1922.
55. Unsigned article, "New Battle of Gettysburg on; Gun Fire Heavy," *The Frederick Post,* June 29, 1922, 1; Unsigned article, "Marines Rehearse Pickett's Famed Gettysburg Charge," June 29, 1922.
56. Unsigned article, "Marines Rehearse Pickett's Famed Gettysburg Charge," June 29, 1922.
57. Frank A. Mallen, "Marines Want 25-Acre Tract for Review Here Saturday," *The Frederick Post,* July 1, 1922, 1.
58. Unsigned article, "Dress Rehearsal for the Charge," June 30, 1922.
59. Unsigned article, "Attack Made on Seminary Ridge," July 1, 1922.
60. Unsigned article, "Attack Made on Seminary Ridge," July 1, 1922.
61. Unsigned article, "Large Attack Is Launched," June 30,

1922.

62. Unsigned article, "Dress Rehearsal for the Charge," June 30, 1922.

63. Raymond S. Tompkins, "Marines on Edge at Gettysburg to Reenact Great Battle Today," July 1, 1922.

64. Unsigned article, "Three Arrested for Bootlegging," *The Gettysburg Times*, July 3, 1922, 1.

65. Unsigned article, "Thirty State Police Here," *Gettysburg Compiler*, July 8, 1922, 1.

66. Unsigned article, "Arrest Camp Followers," *(Gettysburg) Star and Sentinel*, July 8, 1922, 1.

67. Unsigned article, "Officers Visit Carnival," *The Gettysburg Times*, July 12, 1922, 1; Unsigned article, "Legion to Bring Carnival Here," *The Gettysburg Times*, June 9, 1922, 1.

68. Unsigned article, "Has Symptoms of Disease," *The Gettysburg Times*, July 5, 1922, 1.

69. Unsigned article, "Police Close Gambling Games," *The Gettysburg Times*, July 3, 1922, 1.

70. Unsigned article, "Police Close Gambling Games," July 3, 1922, 1.

71. Unsigned article, "Police Close Gambling Games," July 3, 1922, 1.

72. Unsigned article, "Officers Visit Carnival," *The Gettysburg Times*, July 12, 1922, 1.

**CHAPTER 6**

1. R. S. T., "Cemetery Hill Capitulates to Marine Attack," July 5, 1922.

2. Excerpt from a letter from George Pickett to his wife, La Salle, on July 6, 1863. ("Documenting the American South: The Southern Experience in 19th Century America." Documenting the American South: The Southern Experience in 19-th Century America, http://www.docsouth.unc.edu/fpn/pickett/pickett.html, (accessed January 24, 2015.)

3. Unsigned article, "Harding and Pershing View Re-enactment of Pickett's Charge," July 3, 1922; Unsigned article, "Marine Camp is Covered by Mud," *The Gettysburg Times*, July 3, 1922, 1.

4. Unsigned article, "To Receive the President Here," *The Gettysburg Times*, July 1, 1922, 3.

5. Unsigned article, "United States Marines Give Three Demonstrations of Pickett's Charge," *Gettysburg Compiler*, July 8, 1922, 1; Unsigned article, "Pickett's Charge Thrillingly Given before President," *The (Hanover) Evening Sun*, July 3, 1922, 1.

6. Unsigned article, "Pickett's Charge Thrillingly Given before President," July 3, 1922.

7. R. S. T., "Harding to View Marines in New Pickett's Charge," June 30, 1922.

8. Unsigned article, "City Prepares To Welcome The President Here," *The (Frederick) News*, July 1, 1922, 1.

9. Unsigned article, "President Harding To Stop At Schley's Birthplace Today," *The Frederick Post*, July 1, 1922, 1.

10. Unsigned article, "City Prepares To Welcome The President Here," July 1, 1922.

11. Unsigned article, "City Prepares To Welcome The President Here," July 1, 1922.

12. Unsigned article, "City Prepares To Welcome The President Here," July 1, 1922.

13. Unsigned article, "City Prepares To Welcome The President Here," July 1, 1922.

14. Cathy Hunter, "Winfield Scott Schley: A Hero, But Not Without Controversy," National Geographic, December 20, 2012, http://voices.nationalgeographic.com/2012/12/20/winfield-scott-schley-a-hero-but-not-without-controversy (accessed January 28, 2015)

15. Unsigned article, "City Prepares To Welcome The President Here," July 1, 1922.

16. R. S. T., "Pickett's Gettysburg Charge Dramatized in Marine Attack," July 2, 1922.

17. Unsigned article, "Harding Watches Pickett's Charge," New York Times, July 2, 1922, 6; Unsigned article, "President Sees Reproduction of Pickett's Charge," July 2, 1922.

18. Unsigned article, "Harding Party Coming Saturday," *The (Gettysburg) Star and Sentinel*, July 1, 1922, 2.

19. Unsigned article, "Pictures Of Gettysburg Battle Brought To The Sun In Hours," *The (Baltimore) Sun*, July 2, 1922, 3.

20. Unsigned article, "Harding Made Brief Visit Here," July 3, 1922.

21. Unsigned article, "Harding Made Brief Visit Here," July 3, 1922.

22. Unsigned article, "Harding and Pershing View Re-enactment of Pickett's Charge," July 3, 1922; Harry N. Price, "Harding Sees Battle," July 2, 1922; Unsigned article, "Harding Watches Pickett's Charge," *The New York Times*, July 2, 1922, 6.

23. Harry N. Price, "Harding Sees Battle," July 2, 1922.

24. Unsigned article, "Harding Made Brief Visit Here," July 3, 1922.

25. Unsigned article, "Harding and Pershing View Re-enactment of Pickett's Charge," July 3, 1922.

26. George M. Chandler, "Gettysburg, 1922," *Infantry Journal* July (1922), 380.

27. Unsigned article, "President Sees Reproduction of Pickett's Charge," *The Canton Daily News*, July 2, 1922, 1.

28. R. S. T., "Pickett's Gettysburg Charge Dramatized in Marine Attack," July 2, 1922.

29. George M. Chandler, "Gettysburg, 1922," Infantry Journal July (1922); Unsigned article, "Harding and Pershing View Re-enactment of Pickett's Charge," July 3, 1922.

30. George M. Chandler, "Gettysburg, 1922," *Infantry Journal* July (1922).

31. R. S. T., "Pickett's Gettysburg Charge Dramatized in Marine Attack," *Sun*, July 2, 1922.

32. Unsigned article, "President Greets Hanover Children." *The (Hanover) Evening Sun*, July 3, 1922, 3.

33. George M. Chandler, "Gettysburg, 1922," *Infantry Journal* July (1922).

34. R. S. T., "Marines to Begin Rehearsals of Pickett's Charge Today," June 28, 1922.

35. Unsigned article, "General Pickett's Charge Staged for Harding," *New York Tribune*, July 2, 1922, 3.

36. Unsigned article, "Harding and Pershing View Re-enactment of Pickett's Charge," July 3, 1922.

37. R. S. T., "Pickett's Gettysburg Charge Dramatized in Marine Attack," July 2, 1922.

38. George M. Chandler, "Gettysburg, 1922," *Infantry Journal* July (1922).

39. Harry N. Price, "Harding Sees Battle," July 2, 1922.

40. Unsigned article, "Harding and Pershing View Re-enactment of Pickett's Charge," July 3, 1922.

41. R. S. T., "Pickett's Gettysburg Charge Dramatized in Marine Attack," *Sun*, July 2, 1922.

42. Unsigned article, "Harding and Pershing View Re-enactment of Pickett's Charge," July 3, 1922.

43. Unsigned article, "General Pickett's Charge Staged for Harding," July 2, 1922.

44. Unsigned article, "Harding and Pershing View Re-enactment of Pickett's Charge," July 3, 1922.

45. Unsigned article, "Harding Made Brief Visit Here," July 3, 1922.
46. Unsigned article, "Harding Made Brief Visit Here," July 3, 1922.
47. Unsigned article, "Harding Made Brief Visit Here," July 3, 1922.
48. Harry N. Price, "Cheer Harding Party," *The Washington Post*, July 3, 1922, 1.
49. R. S. T., "Pickett's Gettysburg Charge Dramatized in Marine Attack," *Sun*, July 2, 1922.
50. Harry N. Price, "Cheer Harding Party," July 3, 1922; Raymond S. Tompkins, "Marines Plan to Reenact Famous Battle Every Year," July 3, 1922.
51. Harry N. Price, "Cheer Harding Party," July 3, 1922.
52. Unsigned article, "Harding Made Brief Visit Here," July 3, 1922.
53. F. A. Mallen, "Marines Wading Through Water," *The Frederick Post*, July 3, 1922, 1.
54. Unsigned article, "Marine Camp Was Covered by Mud," *The (Gettysburg) Star and Sentinel*, July 8, 1922, 2.
55. Unsigned article, "Marine Camp Was Covered by Mud," July 8, 1922.
56. Unsigned article, "Heard and Seen at Gettysburg," *Leatherneck*, July (1922), 4.
57. R. S. T., "Grandson Sees Marines Enact Pickett's Dash," *The (Baltimore) Sun*, July 4, 1922, 1.
58. Helen Longstreet Dortch, "Rebel Generals' Widows See Pickett Charge Staged," *New York Tribune*, July 4, 1922, 4 ; R. S. T., "Grandson Sees Marines Enact Pickett's Dash," July 4, 1922.
59. R. S. T., "Grandson Sees Marines Enact Pickett's Dash," July 4, 1922.
60. R. S. T., "Grandson Sees Marines Enact Pickett's Dash," July 4, 1922.
61. George M. Chandler, "Gettysburg, 1922," *Infantry Journal* July (1922).
62. Glenn W. LaFantasie, "Joshua Lawrence Chamberlain and the American Dream," *Gettysburg Heroes: Perfect Soldiers, Hallowed Ground* (Bloomington: Indiana UP, 2008), 70.
63. Unsigned article, "Harding Watches Pickett's Charge," July 2, 1922.
64. Raymond S. Tompkins, "Marines on Edge at Gettysburg to Reenact Great Battle Today," July 1, 1922.
65. R. S. T., "Pickett's Gettysburg Charge Dramatized in Marine Attack," *Sun*, July 2, 1922.
66. R. S. T., "Pickett's Gettysburg Charge Dramatized in Marine Attack," July 2, 1922.
67. R. S. T., "Pickett's Gettysburg Charge Dramatized in Marine Attack," *Sun*, July 2, 1922.
68. Unsigned article, "25,000 See Marines Again Reenact Pickett's Charge," *The Washington Post*, July 4, 1922, 2.
69. R. S. T., "Grandson Sees Marines Enact Pickett's Dash," July 4, 1922.
70. Helen Dortch Longstreet, "Longstreet's Widow Tells of Pickett's Last Charge," *New York Tribune*, July 4, 1922, 4.
71. Longstreet, Helen Dortch, "Rebel Generals' Widows See Pickett Charge Staged," July 4, 1922.
72. R. S. T., "Grandson Sees Marines Enact Pickett's Dash," July 4, 1922.
73. Longstreet, Helen Dortch, "Rebel Generals' Widows See Pickett Charge Staged," July 4, 1922.
74. Unsigned article, "'Modern Gettysburg' Fought by Marines in Air Thrillers," *New York Tribune*, July 5, 1922, 3.
75. Unsigned article, "'Modern Gettysburg' Fought by Marines in Air Thrillers," July 5, 1922.
76. R. S. T., "Cemetery Hill Capitulates to Marine Attack,"

77. R. S. T., "Cemetery Hill Capitulates to Marine Attack," July 5, 1922.
78. R. S. T., "Cemetery Hill Capitulates to Marine Attack," July 5, 1922.
79. Unsigned article, "'Modern Gettysburg' Fought by Marines in Air Thrillers," July 5, 1922.
80. R. S. T., "Cemetery Hill Capitulates to Marine Attack," July 5, 1922.
81. F. A. Mallen, "Marines Anxious to Get Back to Fred'k." *The (Frederick) Daily News*, July 6, 1922, 9.
82. R. S. T., "Harding to View Marines in New Pickett's Charge," June 30, 1922.
83. R. S. T., "Pickett's Gettysburg Charge Dramatized in Marine Attack," *Sun*, July 2, 1922.
84. Unsigned article, "Expect Largest Crowd of Cars," *The Gettysburg Times*, n.d., 1.
85. Unsigned article, "United States Marines," July 8, 1922; Unsigned article, "Expect Largest Crowd of Cars," n.d.
86. R. S. T., "Cemetery Hill Capitulates to Marine Attack," July 5, 1922.
87. R. S. T., "Cemetery Hill Capitulates to Marine Attack," July 5, 1922.
88. Unsigned article, "United States Marines," July 8, 1922.
89. Unsigned article, "Marines Thrill 125,000 with Modern Maneuvers," July 5, 1922.
90. Unsigned article, "50,000 See Marines Re-enact 'Pickett's Charge' of July, '63," *Rochester and Democrat Observer*, July 5, 1922.
91. George M. Chandler, "Gettysburg, 1922," *Infantry Journal* July (1922).
92. F. A. Mallen, "Battle of Gettysburg Re-Fought by Marines During Downpour of Rain," *The Frederick Post*, July 5, 1922, 1.
93. R. S. T., "Cemetery Hill Capitulates to Marine Attack," July 5, 1922
94. F. A. Mallen, "Battle of Gettysburg Re-Fought by Marines During Downpour of Rain," July 5, 1922.
95. R. S. T., "Cemetery Hill Capitulates to Marine Attack," July 5, 1922; Unsigned article, "Marines Thrill 125,000 with Modern Maneuvers," July 5, 1922.
96. R. S. T., "Cemetery Hill Capitulates to Marine Attack," July 5, 1922.
97. Unsigned article, "Marines Thrill 125,000 with Modern Maneuvers," July 5, 1922.
98. George M. Chandler, "Gettysburg, 1922," *Infantry Journal* July (1922).
99. Unsigned article, "Marines Thrill 125,000 with Modern Maneuvers," July 5, 1922.
100. F. A. Mallen, "Battle of Gettysburg Re-Fought by Marines During Downpour of Rain," July 5, 1922; George M. Chandler, "Gettysburg, 1922," *Infantry Journal*, July (1922).
101. Unsigned article, "Marines Thrill 125,000 with Modern Maneuvers," July 5, 1922.
102. R. S. T., "Cemetery Hill Capitulates to Marine Attack," July 5, 1922.
103. Unsigned article, "Marines Thrill 125,000 with Modern Maneuvers," July 5, 1922.
104. Unsigned article, "Heard and Seen at Gettysburg," *Leatherneck* July (1922).
105. Unsigned article, "Marines Thrill 125,000 with Modern Maneuvers," July 5, 1922.
106. R. S. T., "Cemetery Hill Capitulates to Marine Attack," July 5, 1922.

107. George M. Chandler, "Gettysburg, 1922," *Infantry Journal* July (1922).
108. George M. Chandler, "Gettysburg, 1922," *Infantry Journal* July (1922).
109. George M. Chandler, "Gettysburg, 1922," *Infantry Journal* July (1922).

**CHAPTER 7**

1. Unsigned article, "Marines Pleased With Frederick," *The (Frederick) News*, July 18, 1922, 3.
2. Unsigned article, "Marine Troops Begin Hike Back to Barracks At Quantico, Virginia," *The Frederick Post*, July 6, 1922, 1.
3. F. A. Mallen, "Marines Anxious to Get Back to Fred'k." July 6, 1922.
4. Unsigned article, "Marines Are Ready To Break Camp," *The (Baltimore) Sun*, July 6, 1922, 7.
5. Unsigned article, "Marines Are Ready To Break Camp," July 6, 1922.
6. F. A. Mallen, "Marines Anxious to Get Back to Fred'k." July 6, 1922.
7. Unsigned article, "Marines Are Ready To Break Camp," July 6, 1922.
8. Unsigned article, "Marines Are Ready To Break Camp," July 6, 1922.
9. F. A. Mallen, "Marines Anxious to Get Back to Fred'k." July 6, 1922.
10. F. A. Mallen, "Marines Anxious to Get Back to Fred'k." July 6, 1922.
11. F. A. Mallen, "Marines Anxious to Get Back to Fred'k." July 6, 1922.
12. Unsigned article, "Marines Enjoy Pool," *The (Gettysburg) Star and Sentinel*, July 15, 1922, 1.
13. Unsigned article, "Marines Enjoy Pool," July 15, 1922.
14. Unsigned article, "Marines To Return To Frederick Today; Review Tomorrow Afternoon," *The Frederick Post*, July 7, 1922, 1.
15. Unsigned article, "Back In White House Again," *The New York Times*, July 9, 1922, 4.
16. Unsigned article, "Hardings, Wed In '91, Mark Anniversary," *The (Baltimore) Sun*, July 9, 1922, 2.
17. Unsigned article, "Marines Bid Adieu To Frederick Cheer," *The (Baltimore) Sun*, July 10, 1922, 2.
18. Unsigned article, "Marines Prepare For Parade Today," The Washington Post, July 12, 1922, 2.
19. Unsigned article, "Foolishness," *The (Gettysburg College) Blister.* June 26, 1922, 1.
20. Unsigned article, "Editorial," *The (Gettysburg College) Blister.* July 6, 1922, 1.
21. Unsigned article, "Marines Prepare For Parade Today," July 12, 1922.
22. Unsigned article, "Marines Prepare For Parade Today," July 12, 1922.
23. Unsigned article, "Marines Back In Washington," The Frederick Post, July 13, 1933, 1.
24. Unsigned article, "Marines Pitch Tents For Night In Daisy Fields Of Maryland," June 21, 1922.
25. Lt. A. S. Bagley, "Letters to the Editor," *The Gettysburg Times*, June 26, 1972, 3.
26. Unsigned article, "Sea Soldiers Not Impressed," *The Gettysburg Times*, July 7, 1922, 1; Unsigned article, "Sea Soldiers Not Impressed," *The (Gettysburg) Star and Sentinel,* July 8, 1922, 1.
27. Unsigned article, "Sea Soldiers Not Impressed," July 7, 1922; Unsigned article, "Sea Soldiers Not Impressed," July 8, 1922.
28. Unsigned article, "Sea Soldiers Not Impressed," July 7, 1922; Unsigned article, "Sea Soldiers Not Impressed," July 8, 1922.
29. Unsigned article, "Sea Soldiers Not Impressed," July 7, 1922; Unsigned article, "Sea Soldiers Not Impressed," July 8, 1922.
30. Unsigned article, "Sea Soldiers Not Impressed," July 7, 1922; Unsigned article, "Sea Soldiers Not Impressed," July 8, 1922.
31. Unsigned article, "Sea Soldiers Not Impressed," July 7, 1922; Unsigned article, "Sea Soldiers Not Impressed," July 8, 1922.
32. F. A. Mallen, "Marines Anxious to Get Back to Fred'k." July 6, 1922.
33. United States Marine Corps, *The United States Marine Band* (Philadelphia: USMC Publicity Bureau, 1927), 7.
34. United States Marine Corps, *The United States Marine Band,* 7.
35. United States Marine Corps, *The United States Marine Band*, 11.
36. United States Marine Corps, *The United States Marine Band*, 11.
37. Lt. Col. Jason K. Fettig, "'The President's Own' United States Marine Band," United States Marine Band, http://www.marineband.marines.mil/About/LibraryandArchives/HailtotheChief.aspx (accessed February 2, 2015).

**PHOTO CREDITS**

pg. 8-9: Courtesy of the U.S. Marine Corps Historical Company.
pg. 10 (bottom): Courtesy of the Library of Congress.
pg. 11: Courtesy of the U.S. Marine Corps Historical Company.
pg. 12-13: Courtesy of the Marine Corps Archives and Special Collections, Ray H. Harrington Collection (COLL/615).
pg. 14 (top): Courtesy of *United States Marine Corps, Marine Barracks, Quantico, Virginia, 1930.*
pg. 14 (bottom): Courtesy of the Library of Congress.
pg. 15: Courtesy of the Marine Corps Association & Foundation.
pg. 16-17: Courtesy of the Library of Congress.
pg. 17: Courtesy of the Library of Congress.
pg. 18 (top): *Leatherneck,* September 2014; "Marines at the Battle of the Wilderness—1921."
pg. 18 (bottom): *A Brief History of the 10ᵗʰ Marines*, 1981.
pg. 19: Courtesy of the U.S. Marine Corps Historical Company.
pg. 20: Courtesy of Marine Corps Archives and Special Collections: Smedley D. Butler Collection (COLL/3124).
pg. 21: Courtesy of the U.S. Naval Institute (U.S. Marine Corps Art Collection).
pg. 22-23: Courtesy of the Marine Corps Archives and Special Collections: John Roth Collection (COLL/941).
pg. 24: Source: Base map from Google Maps.
pg. 25: Courtesy of the Library of Congress.
pg. 26: Courtesy of the Marine Corps Archives and Special Collections, William D. Steeves Collection (COLL/4998).
pg. 27 (top): Courtesy of the Marine Corps Archives and Special Collections.
pg. 27 (bottom): Courtesy of the Marine Corps Archives and Special Collections.
pg. 28: Courtesy of the Library of Congress.
pg. 30: Courtesy of Library of Congress.
pg. 31 (top): Courtesy of Library of Congress.
pg. 31 (bottom): Courtesy of Library of Congress.
pg. 32: Courtesy of the Library of Congress.
pg. 33: Courtesy of ancestry.com.

pg. 34-35: Courtesy of the U.S. Marine Corps Historical Company.

pg. 36: Courtesy of the U.S. Marine Corps Historical Company.

pg 38: Courtesy of the U.S. Marine Corps Historical Company.

pg. 38-39: Courtesy of the U.S. Marine Corps Historical Company.

pg 40: Courtesy of the Marine Corps Archives and Special Collections: Herman Priebe Collection (COLL/1743).

pg. 41: Courtesy of the U.S. Marine Corps Historical Company.

pg. 42 (top): Courtesy of the U.S. Marine Corps Historical Company.

pg. 42 (bottom): Courtesy of the U.S. Marine Corps Historical Company.

pg. 44: Courtesy of Thurmontimages.com.

pg. 45: Courtesy of Thurmontimages.com.

pg. 46: Courtesy of Thurmontimages.com.

pg. 47: Courtesy of Thurmontimages.com.

pg. 48 (top): Courtesy of Thurmontimages.com

pg. 48 (bottom): Courtesy of the Town of Emmitsburg.

pg. 47: Courtesy of the U.S. Marine Corps Historical Company.

Pg. 50-51: Courtesy of the U.S. Marine Corps Historical Company.

pg. 52: Courtesy of the U.S. Marine Corps Historical Company.

pg. 53: Courtesy of the U.S. Marine Corps Historical Company.

pg. 54-55: Photograph by Richard D. L. Fulton.

pg. 56: Photograph by Richard D. L. Fulton.

pg. 57: Courtesy of San Diego Air and Space Museum Archive: Wallace Collection044

pg. 58: Source: The Hospital Corps with the Marine Expeditionary Force in the 1922 Spring Exercises.

pg. 59: Courtesy of the U.S. Marine Corps Historical Company.

pg. 60: Courtesy of Bureau of Engraving and Printing; U.S. Post Office.

pg. 60-61: Courtesy of the U.S. Marine Corps Historical Company.

pg. 62: Courtesy of the U.S. Marine Corps Historical Company.

pg. 63: Courtesy of the U.S. Marine Corps Historical Company.

pg. 64: Courtesy of *The Washington Post*, July 3, 1922, Page 3.

pg. 65: Courtesy of the U.S. Marine Corps Historical Company.

pg. 66: Figure 1. Modified from a base photograph courtesy of the U.S. Marine Corps Historical Company.

pg. 67: Figure 2. Modified from a base photograph courtesy of Google Maps.

pg. 68: Modified from a base photograph courtesy of the U.S. Marine Corps Historical Company.

pg. 69: Courtesy of the U.S. Marine Corps Historical Company.

pg. 70-71: Courtesy of the U.S. Marine Corps Historical Company.

pg. 71: Courtesy of the U.S. Marine Corps Historical Company.

pg. 72: Courtesy of the U.S. Marine Corps Historical Company.

pg. 73: Courtesy of the U.S. Marine Corps Historical Company.

pg. 74-75: Courtesy of Marine Corps Archives and Special Collections: Walter V. Brown Collection (COLL/4326).

pg. 76: Courtesy of the U.S. Marine Corps Historical Company.

pg. 77: Courtesy of the U.S. Marine Corps Historical Company.

pg. 78: Courtesy of Marine Corps Archives and Special Collections: John Helm Collection (COLL/2509).

pg. 79: Courtesy of Marine Corps Archives and Special Collections: Alfred A. Cunningham Collection (COLL/3034).

pg. 80: Courtesy of Marine Corps Archives and Special Collections: Walter V. Brown Collection (COLL/4326).

pg. 81 (top): Source: National Museum of the U.S. Air Force.

pg. 81 (bottom):Courtesy of the U.S. Marine Corps Historical Company.

pg. 82 (top): Courtesy of the U.S. Marine Corps Historical Company.

pg. 83 (bottom): Source: Google maps.

pg. 84: Courtesy of the U.S. Marine Corps Historical Company.

pg. 85: Courtesy of the U.S. Marine Corps Historical Company.

pg. 86 (top): Courtesy of navalwarfare.blogspot.com (NH 99899).

pg. 86 (bottom): Courtesy of the U.S. Marine Corps Historical Company.

pg. 87 (series): Source: San Diego Air and Space Museum Archive: Flickr.

pg. 88: Source: Variety of publications, including *The Brooklyn Standard Union,* June 28, 1922.

pg. 89: Source: *Leatherneck* (Kenneth L. Smith-Christmas, "Marines at the Battle of Gettysburg - 1922," Leatherneck, April 1, 2014, 48-50.)

pg. 91: Courtesy of Marine Corps Association & Foundation.

pg. 92 (top): Courtesy of the U.S. Marine Corps Historical Company.

pg. 92 (bottom): Source: Ancestry.com.

pg. 93 (top): From the *Buffalo Evening News*, June 27, 1922).

pg. 93 (bottom): Source: Ancestry.com.

pg. 94 (top): Photograph by Richard D. L. Fulton.

pg. 95 From the *Buffalo Evening News*, June 27, 1922.

pg. 96-97: Courtesy of the U.S. Marine Corps Historical Company.

pg. 98 (top): Courtesy of the U.S. Marine Corps Historical Company.

pg. 98 (bottom): Courtesy of the Library of Congress.

pg. 99: Courtesy of the Library of Congress.

pg. 100: Courtesy of the Marine Corps Archives and Special Collections.

pg. 101: Courtesy of the U.S. Marine Corps Historical Company.

pg. 102-103: Courtesy of the U.S. Marine Corps Historical Company.

pg. 104 (left): Courtesy of the U.S. Marine Corps Historical Company.

pg. 104 (right): Courtesy of the U.S. Marine Corps Historical Company.

pg. 106 (top):

pg. 106 (bottom):

pg. 107: Courtesy of the U.S. Marine Corps Historical Company.

pg. 108: Courtesy of the Library of Congress.

pg. 109 (top): Courtesy of the Library of Congress.

pg. 109 (bottom): Source: A Brief History of the 10th Marines (David N. Buckner, "Between the Wars," In *A Brief History of the 10th Marines (Washington, D.C.: History and Museums Division, Headquarters, U.S. Marine Corps, 1981*).

pg. 110: Courtesy of the Library of Congress.

pg. 111: Courtesy of the Library of Congress.

pg. 112: Courtesy of the Library of Congress.

pg. 113: Courtesy of the Library of Congress.

pg. 114: Courtesy of the Library of Congress.

pg. 115: Courtesy of the Library of Congress.

pg. 117 (top): Photograph by Richard D. L. Fulton.

pg. 118-119: Courtesy of the Marine Corps Archives & Special Collections.

pg. 120 (top): Courtesy of the Library of Congress.

pg. 120 (bottom): Courtesy of the Library of Congress.

pg. 121: Courtesy of the Marine Corps Archives and Special Collections.

pg. 122 (top): Courtesy of the Library of Congress.

pg. 122 (bottom): Courtesy of the U.S. Marine Corps Historical Company.

pg. 123: Courtesy of the U.S. Marine Corps Historical Company.
pg. 124: Courtesy of the Library of Congress.
pg. 126-127: Courtesy of the U.S. Marine Corps Historical Company.
pg. 128: Courtesy of the U.S. Marine Corps Historical Company.
pg. 130 (top): Courtesy of the Library of Congress.
pg. 130 (bottom): Courtesy of the U.S. Marine Corps Historical Company.
pg. 131: Courtesy of the Library of Congress.
pg. 132-133: Courtesy of the U.S. Marine Corps Historical Company.
pg. 134: Courtesy of the U.S. Marine Corps Historical Company.
pg. 136: Courtesy of the Library of Congress.
pg. 137: Courtesy of the Library of Congress.
pg. 138: Courtesy of the U.S. Marine Corps Historical Company.
pg. 139: Courtesy of the Library of Congress.
pg. 140: Courtesy of the Library of Congress.
pg. 142: Courtesy of the Library of Congress.
pg. 144: Courtesy of the U.S. Marine Corps Historical Company.
pg. 145: Courtesy of the U.S. Marine Corps Historical Company.
pg. 146: Source: Kenneth L. Smith-Christmas, "Marines at the Battle of Gettysburg - 1922," *Leatherneck*, April 1, 2014, 48-50.

pg. 147: Courtesy of Wikimedia Commons.
pg. 148-149: Courtesy of the U.S. Marine Corps Historical Company.
pg. 150 (top): Courtesy of the U.S. Marine Corps Historical Company.
pg. 150 (bottom): Courtesy of the U.S. Marine Corps Historical Company.
pg. 151: Courtesy of the U.S. Marine Corps Historical Company.
pg. 152: Courtesy of the Library of Congress.
pg. 153 (left): Courtesy of the Library of Congress.
pg. 153 (right): Source: *The Blister*, July 6, 1922.
pg. 154: Courtesy of the U.S. Marine Corps Historical Company.
pg. 154-155: Courtesy of the U.S. Marine Corps Historical Company.
pg. 156-157: Courtesy of the Library of Congress.
pg. 158: Courtesy of the Library of Congress.
pg. 160: Courtesy of the Library of Congress.
pg. 161: Courtesy of the Library of Congress.
pg. 162-163: Courtesy of the Library of Congress.
pg. 164 (top): Source: Norval Eugene Packwood, *Leatherhead, the Story of Marine Corps Boot Camp* (Quantico, Va.: Marine Corps Association, 1951).
pg. 164 (bottom): Source: Norval Eugene Packwood, *Leatherhead, the Story of Marine Corps Boot Camp* (Quantico, Va.: Marine Corps Association, 1951).

## Acknowledgements

The authors would like to express their appreciation to Cathe Adelsberger Fulton, wife of co-author Richard D. L, Fulton, who began to amass photographs and information pertaining to the proposed project of writing a book on the current topic four years ago, and who has invested countless hours as the research assistant and copy editor during the completion of *The Last to Fall: The 1922 March, Battles, & Deaths of the U.S. Marines at Gettysburg*.

The authors would also like to thank…

GySgt. Thomas E. Williams, director of the United States Marine Corps Historical Company, for his invaluable assistance with this book, and for proof reading the final draft.

Linda Männik-Richters, Fayetteville, Pennsylvania, for colorizing the cover photograph.

Brent Reidenbach, Lorton, Virginia, for assistance in identification of certain archival photographs.

---

### Want to contribute to future editions?

Do you have photographs, letters, or family stories relating to, or that could relate to, the 1922 Marine maneuvers and reenactments at Gettysburg? The co-authors invite you to solicit any material which may further the record of this unique experience in history. Contact Richard D. L. Fulton at *richardfulton@earthink.net*, or James R. Rada, Jr. at *jimrada@yahoo.com*.

---

# How would the U.S. Marines Have fought the Civil War?

THE SECOND CIVIL WAR

The U.S. Marine Maneuvers & Reenactments of the 1920s and 1930s

By Richard D. L. Fulton & James Rada, Jr.

## Available in 2016

# ABOUT THE AUTHORS

## Richard D. L. Fulton

Richard D. L. Fulton has been involved in journalism and public communications for more than four decades, working in the newspaper industries in New Jersey, Pennsylvania and Maryland, and in communications for the New Jersey Department of Environmental Protection and the U.S. Department of Energy.

He was born in Frederick and grew up in Brunswick, Md., and Rockville, Md., and presently resides in Gettysburg, Pa., with wife Cathe, and four cats, Abby, Coco, Cam, and Little Nipper (named after one of Confederate General Robert E. Lee's cats).

Fulton also has an established record as a lay-professional paleontologist spanning decades. He is recognized as the discoverer of the largest early dinosaur site in Maryland, among his other contributions to the field.

He has won numerous awards for paleontological exhibitions, and most recently received recognition from the Maryland-Delaware-DC Press Association for a series on an ethics investigation.

## James Rada, Jr.

James Rada, Jr. has written many works of historical fiction and non-fiction history. They include the popular books *Saving Shallmar: Christmas Spirit in a Coal Town, Canawlers* and *Battlefield Angels: The Daughters of Charity Work as Civil War Nurses.*

He lives in Gettysburg, Pa., where he works as a freelance writer. James has received numerous awards from the Maryland-Delaware-DC Press Association, Associated Press, Maryland State Teachers Association, Society of Professional Journalists, and Community Newspapers Holdings, Inc. for his newspaper writing.

If you would like to be kept up to date on new books being published by James or ask him questions, he can be reached by e-mail at *jimrada@yahoo.com.*

To see James' other books or to order copies online, go to *www.jamesrada.com.*

If you liked

# THE LAST TO FALL

you can find more stories

at these FREE sites from

## JAMES RADA, JR.

━━━━━━━━━━━━━━━━━━━━━━━━━━━━

## JAMES RADA, JR.'S WEB SITE

### *www.jamesrada.com*

The official web site for James Rada, Jr.'s books and news including a complete catalog of all his books (including eBooks) with ordering links. You'll also find free history articles, news and special offers.

━━━━━━━━━━━━━━━━━━━━━━━━━━━━

## TIME WILL TELL

### *historyarchive.wordpress.com*

Read history articles by James Rada, Jr. plus other history news, pictures and trivia.

━━━━━━━━━━━━━━━━━━━━━━━━━━━━

## WHISPERS IN THE WIND

### *jimrada.wordpress.com*

Discover more about the writing life and keep up to date on news about James Rada, Jr.